STEALING
THE
CORNER
OFFICE

D1566066

STEALING
THE
CORNER
OFFICE

THE WINNING CAREER STRATEGIES
THEY'LL NEVER TEACH YOU
IN BUSINESS SCHOOL

By

BRENDAN REID

CAREER
PRESS

Pompton Plains, NJ

STEALING THE CORNER OFFICE
EDITED BY JODI BRANDON
TYPESET BY EILEEN MUNSON
Cover design by Howard Grossman
Printed in the U.S.A.

To order this title, please call toll-free 1-800-CAREER-1 (NJ and Canada: 201-848-0310) to order using VISA or MasterCard, or for further information on books from Career Press.

CAREER
PRESS

The Career Press, Inc.
220 West Parkway, Unit 12
Pompton Plains, NJ 07444
www.careerpress.com

Library of Congress Cataloging-in-Publication Data

Reid, Brendan.
    Stealing the corner office : the winning career strategies they'll never teach you in business school / by Brendan Reid.
        pages cm
    Includes index.
    Summary: "Stealing the Corner Office is mandatory reading for smart, hardworking managers who always wonder why their seemingly incompetent superiors are so successful. It is a unique collection of controversial but highly effective tactics for middle managers and aspiring executives who want learn the real secrets for moving up the corporate ladder. Unlike virtually all other business books--which are based on the assumption that corporations are logical and fair--Stealing the Corner Office explores the unconventional tactics people less competent than you use to get ahead and stay ahead. It is your proven playbook to thrive and win in an imperfect corporate world"-- Provided by publisher.
    ISBN 978-1-60163-320-0 (paperback) -- ISBN 978-1-60163-441-2 (ebook) 1. Executives--Promotions. 2. Career development. 3. Success in business. I. Title.

HD38.2.R446 2014
658.4'09--dc23

                                                                              2014003194

Author's Note

All company names referenced in this book are fictitious. They are used to make the stories more enjoyable. Any likeness to a real company is accidental.

For my parents,
who gave me the gift of self-belief.
And for Aya,
who taught me the power of dedicating
yourself to something you love.

Acknowledgments

First, thanks to Aya for her unwavering love and support, and to my parents for giving me the personal strength to take on my goals without fear or reservation.

Thanks also to my close friends who were with me before my professional journey even started. I hope you know how much your loyalty means to me.

A special thanks to the managers and executives I've worked with who taught me that there is no single blueprint to success in the human corporation.

Finally, thank you to Arnold who saw potential in my work when many others did not.

Contents

Introduction

I'm afraid to say I spent the first half of my career doing exactly all the wrong things to get ahead. Somewhere in my formative years, like many young managers, I got it into my head that the secret to success came from being smarter, working harder, and executing reliably. I've since learned that these pearls of conventional wisdom are not, in fact, the beacons to success in the corporate world I've come to know. But who could really blame me? The rhetoric is everywhere.

"Be results oriented"—never.

"Hold people accountable"—nope.

"Be passionate about your ideas"—definitely not.

We treat these mantras as gospel and to argue against them is business sacrilege. I dare you to go into your next management meeting and tell the CEO that it's really *not* all about results—see what happens. Walk down the hall and tell your staff that whatever they do, do *not*, under any circumstance present or pursue ideas with too much passion—watch the looks you get. This mindset has been drilled into us decade after decade, school after school, meeting after meeting. It's simply not up for debate—until now, I hope.

It seems every great success story begins with hard work and passion, and ends with fame and fortune.

Margaret Thatcher told us, "I do not know anyone who has gotten to the top without hard work. That is the recipe." The Iron Lady can't be wrong, can she? But then, how does she account for my former boss who thought CAGR[1] was his favorite local radio station? Utterly inept at business analysis, but he had a summer house on Cape Cod. That recipe doesn't sound right, does it?

Colin Powell said, "A dream doesn't become reality through magic; it takes sweat, determination, and hard work." Okay, but what about the operations VP I worked with who thought a scattergraph[2] was some hot new Instagram feature? Zero business acumen, but he made a fortune on the acquisition. Sounds like magic to me.

What took me 15 years to learn is that much of what we hold to be true about success in business is not really true at all. All this rhetoric we honor as fact is mostly just what successful people preach to justify the validity of their own successes. Can you blame them? Nobody goes to sleep at night thanking the heavens they were able to game the corporate system and get ahead in spite of their glaring incompetence. So we recite these half truths about hard work and results orientation and passion to placate ourselves.

After many years of toil and frustration, I've come to realize this long-held perspective is not actually rooted in the reality of modern corporate life, and that following the conventional game plan doesn't give you the best chance to move up the ladder. I'm going to share with you why that is and how you can use this knowledge to your advantage.

Before you dismiss me as a grumpy, old cynic with a case of sour grapes, let me make a few important distinctions. First off, I'm not saying all successful businesspeople are incompetent. There are many smart, successful people out there. I'd venture to say at least half of all the successful executives I know are undeniably intelligent, passionate, and driven. They've followed the classical success playbook to a T and made it work. But here's the thing: I don't think these people have nearly as much to teach us about getting ahead as their equally successful but far less talented other half, the group I lovingly call the "Incompetent Executives."

The temptation will be to label this line of thinking as cynicism. But before you do, take a good look around you and ask yourself honestly who is getting ahead in your company and why.

How many of these executives are intelligent and innovative? How many of them seem inexplicably lucky? And how many of them are actually drooling right now?

In my experience, the fastest path to getting ahead is to learn the secrets of the group we don't like to talk about: the Incompetent Executives—the average and below-average managers who make it big: your idiot boss, the useless marketing VP, your half-witted neighbor, the strategic alliances guy. You know these people as well as I do. "Teflon Executives," a friend of mine calls them. No matter what happens, they always end up on top and yet they seemingly do nothing at all. How are these people getting ahead, and what do they know that you don't? I'm going to let you in on their secrets and give you an inside look at the most important pages from their playbook.

Let me make one thing perfectly clear: I'm not mocking Incompetent Executives—far from it. I hold this group in extremely high regard. In fact, I've been putting their playbook into action for a number of years, and I've seen measurable success in my own career and in the careers of the friends with whom I've shared it. So if you're sitting in your cushy corner office with an average IQ and a fat bank account, I'm not hating on you. In fact, I owe you. The bottom line is, it's a lot more difficult to learn how to become smarter than it is to learn how average and below-average intellects use a unique set of career tactics to get ahead. We're going to steal their secrets to advance our careers.

Interestingly, at this very moment you find yourself in one of the many situations where it pays to think like an Incompetent Executive. The choice in front of you is to a) spend the next five years studying to be a smarter businessperson; you can compete head on with your peers from Harvard and Yale, all executing the same career strategy, or b) spend the next two days reading this book. You will learn how to start winning the game the correct way. Assuming you're willing to humor me a little longer, let me start by providing you some context.

Admittedly I spent the lion's share of my career looking at Incompetent Executives with disdain. I'd joke about them with my fellow colleagues. We'd pontificate about who they had to sleep with to get that job or whose old college buddy they must be. I spent an inordinate amount of time bemoaning the fairness of the situation without giving any real consideration to the more much important question: What are they doing that I can learn from?

I was a classic example of the group I have come to refer to as Smart-but-Stationary Managers. I exhibited all the typical characteristics:

- ⊃ Passionate about my work and ideas.
- ⊃ Hardworking to the point of exhaustion.
- ⊃ Vocal and anxious to debate topics vigorously.
- ⊃ Driven to deliver quarterly results.
- ⊃ Emotionally invested in the company.
- ⊃ Demanding of my employees and co-workers.

On the surface, these seem like great qualities, and at one time, I would have underscored them in my argument about the great injustice of it all. How could I be stuck in middle management when these seemingly incompetent managers continued to rise up the ranks?

And then I started to take that question more seriously. Really—seriously—why are they getting ahead and I am not? What does it actually take to be successful in a corporation? Is being smarter really the smartest way to the top?

Once I started on this train of thought, everything changed for me. I began to see corporate dynamics and career upward mobility in a completely new light. And when I did, some very disturbing evidence began to reveal itself. Many of the qualities I cherished as my strong points were, in actual fact, the very attributes holding me back.

It turns out the qualities I believed were important are not nearly as important as I thought. In some cases, they are counterproductive, and in other cases, they are downright suicidal.

The so-called Incompetent Executive may lack subject matter expertise, work ethic, and professional poise, but he makes up for it in another set of skills architected to advance his career. And it works!

We've all been scoring our skills incorrectly. We need to reset how we assign value to our behaviors and priorities as managers. And that's why as much as the term Incompetent Executive sounds derogatory, I promise you it's not. This group of executives has figured out how to get ahead without many of the skills most of us hold so proudly. They have a lot to teach us.

I wrote this book knowing that some readers and critics will dismiss it as cynicism. They will point to a hundred cases where smart, hardworking people are successful. They are missing the point. The purpose of this book is to very seriously examine the behaviors and tactics that enable a specific group of average and below-average managers to succeed and thrive within corporations today, and to curate a set of lessons from them that talented managers can add to their arsenals and finally reach their potential in the corporate world.

More and more, our corporations and governments seem to be run by people whose only perceivable talent is in knowing how to win. My goal with this book is to arm the talented and competent with a new perspective and tool set to do just that—win. Cynical or not, we all observe these patterns on a daily basis, and we owe it to ourselves to stop asking the wrong questions and start asking the right ones.

Chapter 1

Your Playing Field: Dispelling the Myth of Meritocracy

The biggest reason talented managers don't advance as quickly as they should is that they don't fully understand the playing field. We make false assumptions about corporate dynamics, causing us to build suboptimal strategies for our advancement.

A good starting point is some clarity on how corporations really operate and what really drives decision-making in a company. We all want to believe companies act with logic and fairness. We want to believe they identify and reward hard work, talent, and passion with career advancement. We build our career strategies based upon these assumptions. Unfortunately, that is not how corporations work in reality.

The Corporation I Know

In this first chapter, we're going to look at a set of little known, albeit universal, corporate dynamics that stand in stark contrast to the widely held perceptions of how companies operate. These dynamics conspire to make conventional career tactics ineffective. They are the reason hard work, reliability, and talent do not, in and of themselves, form a winning strategy in the corporate world I know. In actual fact, most corporations function in a manner that actually favors the Incompetent Executive. Let's examine the playing field more closely so we can build a career strategy designed to win in the real environment we're playing in.

We speak about companies with a certain assumed respect for operational integrity and logic. The media reports on corporate strategy and execution as though they're mechanical and well-conceived. But it doesn't take more than about six months working in middle management inside a typical corporation to realize that all companies are badly flawed from top to bottom. On the inside we see just how bad things really are. Companies I've worked with almost universally operate with no logic or memory whatsoever. Let me give you some classic examples:

Every couple of years, we need to retrain the sales force on some new selling methodology so we don't have to admit we have hired weak talent.

Every three years, it's mandatory to re-launch the partner program to let the world know you're a partner-friendly company—that will make all the difference.

And at least once every five years, we need to bring all the regional teams under one global umbrella under the guise of building international go-to-market consistency.

It's a ridiculous cycle, ostensibly about building excellence, but in reality about saving face and distributing blame.

Launching the new sales partner program is not about improving distribution or market share. It's about deflecting failure toward some faceless program instead of at ourselves. Retraining the sales force is not about making them more effective. It's about buying a few more quarters before we get fired. Juggling reporting structures has nothing to do with globalization or brand consistency. It's about demonstrating a reason other than incompetence for our failure. We make these decisions because we are human. Logic and merit are not the driving forces.

Corporations, after all, are comprised of people, and people care about personal security over everything else—just ask Maslow.[1] People are also not logical by nature; they're instinctive. They opt for self-preservation over and above any notion of corporate allegiance. This is why companies execute completely in spite of themselves. They make bad decision after bad decision at a micro level, and then launch big changes and programs to simultaneously excuse and correct them. Although this reality can be disturbing, it has major implications on your strategy for career success.

Early on in our careers, we assume a certain logical order of things in business. We use terms like *meritocracy*[2] to describe how things *should* work. Should? Yes. Do? No. If a widespread corporate meritocracy exists, then the scoring system it uses runs counter to any rational definition of merit. With this backdrop in mind, you can see why an unconventional approach to your career might begin to make sense.

We all have examples of half-witted executives who reap all the trimmings of success with seemingly no perceivable talent or passion. We tell ourselves it's unfair or that it's an aberration, or that one day our hard work will pay off. But that's the wrong way to look at the phenomenon. Instead of dismissing the Incompetent Executive, and blindly continuing with the same formula that got us to where we are, we need to look a little deeper at their behaviors. We need to steal their secrets for our own career playbooks.

How They Get In

When your company first started, it probably wasn't full of Incompetent Executives. More than likely, it was started by a few very smart, savvy, and energetic professionals with a great vision. So then, why now, when you look around, do you see so many executives who seem to have magically risen to the top without much in the way of expertise or enthusiasm?

It starts with the way companies hire and manage people through the corporate hierarchy. After all, if companies didn't hire and promote Incompetent Executives, this phenomenon wouldn't exist. At the risk of oversimplifying, the basic human need for self-preservation is the catalyst for a set of illogical human resource practices that create an entry point and incubator for Incompetent Executives. Let me walk you through a few of our most important and flawed hiring principles.

"Fit With the Team"

When it comes to hiring, "fit" is a farcical rationale that benefits Incompetent Executives at the expense of Smart-but-Stationary Managers. If you see an Incompetent Executive in your company, it's highly likely they were hired or promoted because they were a good fit. This is a common line of misguided thinking we use to make hiring people we like on a personal level seem like sound business logic. Every day, we see companies hire and fire for fit. We read stories about Google and Facebook, and half pipes and graffiti artists, and we use these images of cultural harmony to justify suboptimal hiring choices.

When we hire, we instinctively want to avoid people who are smarter than we are and who could threaten our success. That is a very human aspect of human resources we too often ignore. We gravitate toward people who will make us happier and make our existence more enriching. So we hire people like us. The result is companies make bad hiring decisions over and over again, applying the same flawed logic. Making matters worse, this so-called logic also assumes "fit with our culture" is actually a good thing. That philosophy is based on the far-fetched assumption that the current culture is actually positive and one we want to reproduce. As it happens, I've worked at two truly toxic companies that spouted the principle of "maintaining our culture" like a religion, even though it was obvious that the culture being fought so hard to preserve was inherently dysfunctional.

"Fit with the team" is a never-ending cycle, as you can surmise. We hire incompetent people because they will be a great fit. Then we repeat over and over and over again, as fitting with incompetence begets more incompetence. The culture inevitably becomes one designed to feed mediocrity instead of meritocracy.

"The Consensus Choice"

Consensus hiring can kill a company, but it's great if you're an Incompetent Executive. I don't know exactly when it began, but these days you can't bring anyone on board without four or five additional people interviewing the candidate and ulti-mately signing off.

It is always easy to find a reason why one more person should have input into a hiring decision. Some companies, who oversubscribe to dotcom human resources best practices, go to extremes in support of consensus hiring. A friend of mine recently had to interview in front of a 25-person panel to get a check-in job at WestJet Airlines. This is the epitome of mis-guided consensus hiring. What are the chances 25 people could ever agree on a truly transformative candidate? In practice, large group hiring always favors the most likeable candidate or the candidate least likely to create discomfort or change.

Somewhere along the way, we've distorted much of the great thinking by Patrick Lencioni[3] and other organizational behavior leaders who espouse the value of maintaining con-trols over who comes into the company. We tell ourselves that having more people comfortable with a candidate means they are more likely to be a positive addition to the culture. But this is flawed logic. In practice, hiring by consensus accomplishes precisely the opposite of what it's attempting to emulate.

Ask yourself honestly: When did group consensus ever deliver real greatness? And let me make an important distinc-tion: I'm speaking about consensus not collaboration; they're very different animals.

We've all seen the Asch research studies[4] where a group of five people is sent into a room. They are presented several line segments; they are obviously different lengths. Prior to entering the room, the moderator tells four of the individu-als to lie about which line is longer. When the four confeder-ates shockingly point to the shorter line, the unknowing fifth guy reluctantly agrees. Nearly 35 percent of candidates tested conformed at least once with an obviously incorrect answer. Groups don't make good choices. Groups for collaboration—yes, groups for decision making—no.

By the same logic it stands to reason if five people interview a group of candidates you're going to see conformity in action. You will get a decision that is the least disruptive to the current team and the most serving to the interests of the voters' own careers. With consensus hiring you'll rarely get a candidate who will push the team to the next level or cause healthy conflict. You will rarely get what's best for the company. All we accomplish through consensus hiring is to multiply the human self-preservation dynamic—favoring the Incompetent Executive once again.

"More Experienced"

Experience is a word we too often misuse to justify hiring weak talent to protect us when they inevitably fail. We fall back on experience because identifying real talent in people is too hard. In practice, however, the most experienced candidate is almost never the best candidate. In fact, one of the most common characteristics I see in Incompetent Executives is over-qualification. Too much experience should be a hiring red flag, but in most cases it serves as a trap for hiring committees and managers. Most Incompetent Executives have a lot of experience, but not the good kind, I can assure you. It's the kind of experience companies mistakenly over-value, over and over again. Let me give you an example.

I'll post a job opening for a mid-level marketing coordinator and gather a variety of candidates for consideration. Each person involved in the hiring decision will review resumes and perform a basic level of due diligence. Without fail, everyone will point to the candidate with 15 years' experience as the obvious choice. I want nothing to do with this candidate. More often than not, the most significant thing this candidate will bring to the table is rigidity. Clearly they have not demonstrated the flexibility, leadership, or talent to advance beyond this level. But as clear as this is to me, nobody else thinks this way. Nine times out of 10, the inept (albeit experienced) candidate gets the job.

Overvaluing experience in hiring very much follows the old purchasing axiom: "Nobody ever got fired for buying IBM." Hiring the most experienced candidate is the safe play. And people make defensive hiring decisions. You can't get faulted for choosing the candidate everybody knew was most experienced—so you do it. You tell yourself the less experienced but more talented candidate was a little green or would require too much hand-holding. In our hearts, we know this is untrue but we do it anyway. And so, the perpetual cycle favoring the Incompetent Executive continues.

How They Get to the Top

Our first three examples focused on hiring practices because that is what kick-starts the flow of people through the corporate food chain. These examples showed how Incompetent Executives get into the organization in the first place. Let me give you a few more examples. This time, we'll dig into how promotions occur and how vacancies are filled. Again we will see some very human corporate dynamics at play that favor the Incompetent Executive.

"Promote from Within"

"Promoting from within" is a policy disguised as employee loyalty but is really about cost and conflict avoidance. It is most widespread at the executive level where recruitment costs and scrutiny are highest. It is very common to see companies promote an internal employee without conducting a serious external candidate search when vacancies exist. I would go so far as to say it's the predominant behavior in practice. If you've ever interviewed for a job but couldn't shake the feeling they already had an internal candidate selected, you'll know what I'm talking about.

On the one hand, "promote from within" can have some clear benefits for staff morale and motivation. It's good for the company to demonstrate feasible career mobility for employees. On the other hand, much of the time when we opt for internal promotion without a serious external search, we favor the Incompetent Executive once again.

Though the "promote from within" policy masquerades as beneficial for employees, the question is, Which employees does it actually benefit? In my experience "promote from within" only perpetuates the very same hiring mistakes that cause incompetent people to get into the organization in the first place. "Consensus," "experience," and "fit" are all equally misapplied in the promotion scenario as well. The result is the Incompetent Executive gets promoted, and the Smart-but-Stationary Manager gets left behind.

"Hit the Ground Running"

"Hit the ground running" is fundamentally flawed as a rationale for promotion. It takes a ridiculously short-term perspective on staffing. Ridiculous or not, we've all heard this line a thousand times, and if you're honest with yourself, you've probably said it a few times, too. Against any logic I can muster, "hit the ground running" seemingly values the first 30 to 90 days over the balance of an entire career.

How many times have you heard managers justify promoting an inferior candidate based on how fast the person can "hit the ground running"? I've probably heard it three times in the last six months. We fool ourselves into thinking some magic is going to happen in the first 90 days. But have you ever seen that happen in practice? In reality, a candidate cannot create meaningful change within 90 days unless he or she is reckless and the change is negative.

"Hit the ground running" favors familiarity over effectiveness. But when has familiarity ever led to growth or evolution? The most familiar candidates are too often part of the problem in the first place. But as much as it baffles the mind, this is a ubiquitous practice that favors the Incompetent Executive once again. Rather than diligently search for the most talented candidate, we promote someone we're comfortable with. And so the Incompetent Executive moves up another rung on the corporate ladder.

"Top Contributor to Manager"

Corporations have a natural predisposition to promote top individual contributors into management positions. This is the reason you can never figure out how the airhead from your high school is running your global sales organization. This practice is very common in sales and engineering, and I've seen it cripple more than one company.

For some reason, we always feel pressure to promote great individual stars. You know who they are: the coding wizard who knows every inch of your technology and spent most of last year living in his mom's basement, the smooth-talking sales guy who crushes his quota every quarter and has bedded most of the strippers on the Eastern seaboard. Inevitably, we promote these people into management roles against our better judgment. We relegate them from valuable contributors into incapable managers. In some misguided sense of obligation, we "reward" great individual performers with management responsibilities—much of the time against their own wishes.

We must believe deep down inside that if a great individual contributor is leading a team, some amount of his or her mojo is bound to trickle down to the staff. But inevitably we see trickle-down mojo proven to be inherently flawed. Great individual contributors very often make poor managers. The personal mojo they possess rarely trickles down through the team. This is a case where the dynamics of a corporation actually work to transform competent contributors into Incompetent Executives.

Okay, Now What?

What we've seen so far is that the very human nature of companies creates the breeding ground for successful albeit Incompetent Executives. This is in stark contrast to how mechanical and logical the media portrays corporations to be. But it's also no less true, as your own personal experience will tell you. Any notion of meritocracy you may have held needs to go out the window.

So now the question becomes, If companies make hiring and promotion decisions in a way that puts passionate, innovative, intelligent people at a disadvantage, how do we turn the game back in our favor?

Chapter 2

Your Mindset: Why You Have All the Wrong Priorities

Your number-one goal when you are at work should be to advance your career. Too many of us take a passive approach to career management. We mistakenly assume the company will eventually recognize and reward our hard work and talent. And so we spend our time working on the wrong priorities based on this false assumption. As we've seen, corporations in practice don't favor a career strategy that relies on merit alone. We need to change our priorities so we can actively advance our careers.

For many years I fell victim to this career-management trap. I focused on all the wrong things. For me, the number-one priority in the first part of my career was to deliver results. I was rarely late. I delivered projects with quality and I never strayed from my quarterly objectives. Performance was my *raison d'être* and I would focus as much as 90 percent of my time on this aspect of my career. A distant second on the priority list was mastering my craft. I probably allocated 5 percent of my time to this. For me, that craft was marketing, and if I had a spare moment here and there, I'd spend it learning to be a better marketer. But I almost never ventured outside of my core area of expertise. My final 5 percent was spent relationship-building, which I focused at my own level of the corporate hierarchy, building a network of peers. In hindsight I know these were largely the wrong priorities. At best they were out of balance with one another. The logical next question is, Why?

What's Good for the Goose?

If you are anything like I was during the first part of my working life, you're concentrating on the wrong priorities at work, too. It's very likely you're too focused on execution and you're not nearly focused enough on career advancement. Let's be clear that these are absolutely not the same thing—execution and advancement. The difference, though appearing subtle at first, is important to understand. Execution is fundamentally about meeting company objectives. Advancement is fundamentally about meeting your personal objectives. Although we might want to believe that achieving one will inevitably lead to achieving the other, this is not often the case in practice.

I'm sorry to be the bearer of bad news, but your company doesn't really care about your advancement. The company's number-one priority is delivering shareholder value. In fact, anything else would be against the law in most commercial scenarios. Shareholder value is the corporation's ultimate decision-making north star. It's the justification it uses to explain mass layoffs, restructuring, and all the rest of the things companies do that are at odds with employee personal well-being. But don't get me wrong, I'm not arguing against this practice. I want the companies I own stock in to behave this way. They're right to do so. We're the misguided ones. We're the ones who go into work every day trying to do our best to put the company first, to rally together with our colleagues, to beat the competition, and to build a great organization. We've got it wrong.

But if the company's top priority is shareholder value, shouldn't your top priority also be shareholder value? That, of course, depends on which shareholders we're talking about. The mistake most of us make is to assume the shareholders we should care about are the same shareholders the corporation cares about. Your number one concern should be *your* shareholders: you, your spouse, your kids, your pets. These are the people who have invested in you, not the bankers and venture capitalists and high-volume traders on Wall Street.

Yes, your company may have issued you stock options to try to align your personal interests with the corporate objectives, but it still doesn't change the most important point. Your driving objective should be advancement, not execution. With advancement comes money and benefits and vacation time and retirement savings. Execution doesn't guarantee you anything unless people notice and reward you for it. And they often won't. The company as an entity may benefit from you executing effectively, but the individual human beings who make up the company are pursuing individual human agendas. Individuals care about self-preservation, job security, and their own advancement. Your execution is not what motivates them on a daily basis. The rub lies in the fact they ultimately form the decision-making engine for the corporation. Entities don't make decisions; people do. They determine your upward mobility or your ultimate termination. A career strategy based solely on achieving the objectives of the corporation is a losing one. It works against the human corporate dynamics instead of with them.

A Rising Tide?

Your company's success is not a prerequisite for your personal success. This can be a hard truth to accept, but waking up to that reality changes the way you work and the way you embrace change, both positive and negative. I can tell you from my personal experience, most of my own career advancement has come in times of corporate failure, not success. And this principle is a key weapon in the arsenal of the Incompetent Executive who inexplicably rises through the ranks while you tread water. They genuinely do not care about the company's success or failure, and neither should you.

But what about the principle of rising tides lifting all ships, you might ask? If the company is successful, won't we all be successful too? To this I make the underused "bear case" counter-argument: *I don't need to outrun the bear; I only need to outrun you.* In my own experience more opportunities are actually presented when the company is not successful than when it is. Think about that for a moment. If the company is doing well and the rising tide is raising all ships, then you're never getting ahead of your own competition—the other managers at your level in the company. You're rising proportionally; you're not winning. You need a certain amount of failure in the company to create tactical opportunities to advance your position. The company's competition is not your competition. Your competition is your peers, and you have to outplay them to win.

This is another difficult concept for most smart, conscientious people to get behind but one that makes the Incompetent Executive such a formidable opponent. While you're wasting your time and energy helping the company succeed, he's looking for failures to swoop in and save the day. He's advancing and you're waiting. The sad truth is the best career strategy is actually based on capitalizing on times of turmoil and not on rooting for consistent company success. When you reorient yourself to this way of thinking, you need to reassess whether or not you're actually playing the game correctly. What does this say about the way you allocate your time or how you approach your work or how you view your colleagues? If an execution focus isn't a winning strategy, then what is?

How Do We Win?

There is a fundamental difference between executing a winning career strategy and working hard. Your priorities need to reflect this. This is a book about winning—about actually getting ahead. So if you're feeling a little uneasy about where this is going, I suggest this is a good place to bail. A winning career strategy is about playing the best game you can with the hand you're dealt and knowing the players you're up against. It's not a game that can be played in a vacuum, as the textbooks and conventional wisdom would have you believe. In the sections to follow we'll look at the players in the game. We'll profile some of the most common types of Incompetent Executives, Smart-but-Stationary Managers, and a sad group I call the Lost Souls. This is where we start understanding your competition.

Chapter 3

Your Competition: Who's Really Getting Ahead in Your Company?

Now that we understand the playing field and the mindset you need to succeed, it's time to meet your competition. Many managers don't view their colleagues and peers as competitors, but that is exactly what they are in the game of career advancement. There are a finite number of promotions available and many possible candidates. Very often we have to wait several years for one opportunity to move up the ladder, so we need a winning strategy to make sure we beat out the competition.

Winning, as we've discussed, is not determined in practice by talent or work ethic. At the very least, these virtues cannot advance your career on their own. The winners come in all shapes and sizes, and achieve victory using a wide variety of techniques. In fact, only half of the successful executives I've worked with are competent when measured in conventional terms. The other half get there a different way.

Who Are These People?

Now it's time to take a good look around the executive table at your company. How many of these people would you want taking your SAT over for you? How many of them got here because they deliver results and show true passion for their work? How many of them seem utterly incompetent, morally questionable, and intellectually challenged?

Now pause for a moment, because this is when we normally start in with the hypotheticals and self-delusion:

> *"Well, maybe he's delivering and I just don't see it."*

> *"Well, if keep working hard I'll get there, too."*

> *"Well, good things come to those who wait."*

If you were wandering down that train of thought, I'm telling you as a friend you're asking all the wrong questions. The better questions are:

> *"What are these people doing that I should be emulating?"*

> *"If it works this well for them, what could it do for a smart guy like me?"*

> *"How can I learn to do what they do?"*

If it only happened once in a while, we could dismiss the phenomenon of the Incompetent Executive as an anomaly. The problem is it's the rule, not the exception. When I look back at the executive boardrooms from my former workplaces, without question I see some legitimate stars, but they're surrounded by the cast of *Three's Company*. If hard work and results are the keys to success, this phenomenon should not exist. Something doesn't add up.

Where Do They Live?

You might ask, "Does he just work for really bad companies?"

Fair question. And truth be told, I've worked for a couple of the worst companies out there. But I've also worked for some great companies, including two that were successfully sold for massive profits. The truth is I've worked for all types of companies and I've consulted for many more. Big companies, small companies, tiny startups—it's all the same. Everywhere you work, you will find a disproportionate number of highly paid executives who achieve success in spite of limited talent, passion, and work ethic.

Assuming your own experiences look something like mine, ask yourself again: Why have these people achieved the level of success they have?

One reason, as we saw in the first chapter, is that the corporate environment itself incubates and feeds this phenomenon. It's in the DNA. The way in which companies make decisions actually creates a breeding ground for the mediocre and a safe haven for the incompetent to live and thrive.

The other reason is that Incompetent Executives have developed a special set of tactics designed to be successful in this environment. Their tactics are well-honed, and they don't rely on scarce virtues like talent and intellect to be successful. They're the group in the game playing to win. The rest of us are playing to survive. We're going to examine the three most common Incompetent Executive profiles. We'll delve deep into their mindsets and maneuvers to understand how they get ahead in spite of their limitations. And we'll steal their best strategies and put them into our own

Stealing the Corner Office

playbooks. But before we get to them, let's spend some time better understanding ourselves.

Line 'Em Up

In this next section, we'll take a closer look at Smart-but-Stationary Managers. They'll help us to understand and assess the weakness of our current approach before we build our new playbook.

3 Smart-but-Stationary Managers

Having been one for so long, I feel a certain connection with the Smart-but-Stationary Manager. We're that perpetually frustrated lot who just can't understand why our tireless efforts, keen intellect, and passion aren't enough to get ahead in the company. We are not to be confused with the Lost Souls who I will profile next. Lost Souls sadly have little or no chance of ever getting ahead. By contrast, Smart-but-Stationary Managers have all the potential in the world; they're just playing the game incorrectly.

During the past five years, I've studied the Smart-but-Stationary species, segmenting it into three profiles. There are similarities across profiles, but each one has its own special flaw that makes it uniquely well suited to a lifetime of career stagnation. Smart-but-Stationary Managers come in various shapes and sizes, but consistently exhibit characteristics from one of three classic profiles:

    ⊃   The Go-to Guy.

    ⊃   The Passion Player.

    ⊃   The Task Master.

The Go-To Guy

Our first profile is the Go-to Guy, or Go-to Girl as the case may be. Many readers will find themselves in this group. It's a very tempting role to play because it comes with perks along the way and disguises itself as an active career strategy. I can assure you it is not.

Go-to Guys can always be counted on to come through in a jam. They will work tirelessly through a problem, roll up their sleeves, and solve the issue of the day. They're rocks. These individuals are a fundamental part of the corporate engine and every executive has at least one on his or her team. The weaker the boss is at execution, the more he or she relies on a Go-to Guy.

At first glance, you might think being a Go-to Guy would be good for your career. Whether it is or it isn't depends on where you're setting the bar. If you're looking for job security, then by all means be a Go-to Guy. Latch yourself onto an executive and solve small problems for the rest of your career. If you're lucky enough to attach yourself to the right manager, you might even move up the corporate ladder—eventually. This is a career strategy akin to those little fish that attach themselves to sharks. However, if you've set the bar higher and you want to become successful in your own right, being a Go-to Guy is a dead end.

First off, as a Go-to Guy, your career success and failure is far too dependent on the success and failure of the executive you serve. These roles often masquerade as mentorships. You're the right hand to the boss. You tell yourself it will pay off one day when he or she moves up the corporate ladder. And though that can occasionally happen, it's certainly not an active career management strategy you can control. And heaven forbid you attach yourself to the wrong manager; you can literally waste three to five years riding alongside the wrong fish.

Secondly, in this role, you will never change the prevailing go-to dynamics even if you do advance your career. Yes, you may slowly creep up the ladder behind your boss. But that's it. The Go-to Guy is given lots of opportunity to contribute but almost no opportunity for leadership—certainly no visible leadership, which is the only kind that counts. Your current role is a long audition for your desired role. It's about perceptions. If you never have the opportunity to lead, you never position yourself as a potential leader in the minds of the people who will ultimately influence your upward mobility.

Finally, being a Go-to Guy can limit lateral movement as well, which is often a precursor to upward advancement. At one point in my own career, after having served loyally as the Go-to Guy for an executive, I learned that it had been suggested I take on more responsibility in another department. My mentor, who couldn't bear the possibility of losing his loyal servant, shut down the idea. He said I was too valuable where I was and probably not ready yet for my own team. If you're a Go-to Guy, you can bet your boss is also not actively looking for opportunities for you to move to other parts of the organization. I actually caught myself recently thinking this way about one of my best employees. As ugly as it sounds, it's just human nature. None of us are immune.

The trap of the Go-to Guy role is that it actually feels quite good. Everyone likes to be needed. And there are certain trimmings along the way, like opportunities to sit in on a board meeting or present to a top client. These special treats make us feel important. And worse, they create the illusion of progress and success. But I'm sorry to say for all you Go-to Guys and Girls, they really are only illusions. Playing this role is actually slowing your career advancement and tying you unnecessarily to someone whose self-interest is not served by having you move up and away.

The Passion Player

The second Smart-but-Stationary profile is the Passion Player. The Passion Player has become more common as we've started to collectively idolize the iconic entrepreneurs like Steve Jobs and Mark Zuckerberg. In my opinion, this can be one of the most dangerous roles to play in your career. Many of us imagine ourselves as the next transformative innovator, so we play the role in our day-to-day jobs in hopes one day we'll be recognized for our vision and strategy. Very early in my career, I played this role and never understood why everyone thought I was a jerk and why I never got ahead. Although it's not as common as the Go-to Guy, it's twice as deadly to your career. Unlike the Go-to Guy approach, which can lead to career stagnation, the Passion Player strategy can lead to career disintegration. Though I've long since abandoned the passion strategy, I see it in my partner and we work together to keep it in check.

Let me describe the Passion Player for you with a hope you don't see many of these characteristics in yourself, because they can be detrimental to your career. The Passion Player always has an idea, or strategy, or vision for the company and will climb up the tallest mountain to shout it out for the world to hear. Think Jerry Maguire. They spend their lives debating their idea with others. They drag people to meetings, argue about the rightness or wrongness of their idea, and search out budget and support and alignment for *their* idea. And they gripe and complain to coworkers about why nobody gets it.

Getting emotionally attached to your own ideas and projects is not a winning game plan. With very few exceptions, the most successful people in corporations are the analysts, not the passionates. The managers who win in the end are able to debate both sides of every idea regardless of who generated it, and then support all outcomes equally. They cultivate an image of objectivity rather than passion, which in my experience is much more useful in your career.

The temptation is to fall into the trap of caring about who is right at the expense of what is right—and to be more precise, what is right for your career. I've seen many passionate managers fight to the death for an idea. Only after paying the price did they wonder if it was really worth it. The Incompetent Executive, I can assure you, does not care about any one idea. But she's on the winning side of every decision.

The biggest reason the Passion Player's strategy is a mistake is that it's just too risky. Your upside with this strategy is that you might think up some truly great ideas, and people will value them enough to both excuse your behavior and promote you. But that so rarely happens in practice. On the flip side, your emotional attachment and dogged evangelism of an idea will almost certainly cause disruption. They will alienate you from the people who ultimately influence your success. The Passion Player strategy is a classic negative expected value proposition.

When I talk to friends and clients about career strategies, this topic is one of the most controversial. I get pushback every time:

> "Are you seriously advocating against being passionate about your work?

> "Are you telling me that Steve Jobs didn't get emotional about his ideas?"

> "I saw the Facebook movie, and Zuckerberg's entire life was consumed by his passion. He ran over people to achieve his vision. It worked out pretty well for him, didn't it?"

For starters, 99.999 percent of us are not Steve Jobs or Mark Zuckerberg, so we shouldn't be adopting their career strategies. We need to choose a winning strategy for our careers. Let me repeat that: a *winning* strategy. Your career is a game and you can play it any way you want. Just because something worked for Jobs doesn't mean it's the best strategy for you. The Passion Player strategy, while tempting, is more likely to leave you in the unemployment line than the executive suite.

The Task Master

The final Smart-but-Stationary Manager is the Task Master. This is not a profile we would naturally associate with career stagnation. In fact, much has been written to the contrary about the power of making enemies in business and on the importance of driving accountability. As the name suggests, the Task Master is demanding. This is the manager who drives people hard. She demands accountability and pushes everyone around her to perform. The Task Master embraces conflict in all its forms and is results oriented literally to a fault.

The Task Master is near and dear to my heart. Not because I see attributes in myself (if anything, I'm too passive), but I see them in spades in my partner. She is a classic Task Master, and it worked against her for many years. I should make one caveat up front: There are some corporations where a Task Master can thrive, but they're rare and found in specific industries only. My partner developed her Task Master approach working in the fashion publishing industry. She honed her skills and management approach in this business for more than a decade—picture *The Devil Wears Prada*. This is a cutthroat industry where the world revolves around deadlines, quality of work is heavily scrutinized, and the players are inherently critical. Now imagine working in this industry for a decade and moving over to a 50-year-old retail company or some young startup technology firm and executing the same tactics. It's a recipe for career disaster.

Though the Task Master's strategy may play well in the fashion business, it absolutely does not work in your typical company for several reasons. Reason number one is that most corporations are comprised primarily of mediocre talents. Your own experience will confirm this. And because people are motivated by their own self-preservation, the mediocre ones, when they form the majority, create a culture that fights against the very things Task Masters stand for. When the nonperformers outnumber the performers, things like holding people accountable and driving people to results become counter-culture. This means Task Masters are always fighting against the grain, making it extremely difficult to get ahead.

My partner was once placed on a performance-improvement plan for creating conflict at work, even though her actual performance was documented as exemplary. I've actually seen this happen a couple of times in companies, and most of the time the conflict in question is entirely professional. But in the modern corporate environment "holding people account-able" can often become "creating conflict." "Driving people to results" can morph into "difficult to work with." There is a very low tolerance for healthy conflict in most companies, despite what they might want to believe. It's truly a sad real-ity of the modern corporation, one many of us underestimate. Knowing this means that if you're a Task Master or have Task Master tendencies, you have to change your game unless you find yourself in one of the few industries where hardball man-agement is condoned.

Through the years, I've observed my partner go through a variety of challenges at work. We talk about how critical it is to separate what you feel *should* be the way to manage with what is actually the *optimal* way to manage to advance your career. Yes, your coworkers should be trying to do what's best for the company. Yes, they should be driving hard to perform on every task. But when has this ever been true in practice? No company is like this. Companies, for the most part, are com-prised of people who just want a happy life, to have job secu-rity, and to get home at a reasonable hour every night. Most people aren't pushing themselves to perform and don't want to be pushed by you.

So if you're a Task Master and you're wondering why you're not getting ahead, it's because you make people uncom-fortable. They don't like working with you. And, as long as there are more of them than there are of you, you'll never get anywhere. People inherently want to work with people similar to themselves and who they like. Any strategy for managing a career that includes not being liked by others is flawed. One thing I know for certain is that most all the Incompetent Executives I've known are extremely likeable people who rarely, if ever, push others hard at work.

———

There's a good chance you saw attributes of yourself in one or more of these Smart-but-Stationary Manager profiles. And, depending on the industry you're in and the company you work for, some will cost you more than others. Without question, though, these attributes are at best neutral for your career. They're certainly not accelerating your success. So if you did find yourself in the Task Master or the Passion Player or the Go-to Guy, take solace. You have all the potential you need to advance your career. In the sections that follow, we'll assemble a winning playbook that will complement your raw talent with the best tactics employed by the Incompetent Executive. This combination will make you unstoppable.

Next, we'll look at three Incompetent Executives. We will start to see how they apply a unique set of tactics designed to get ahead in a corporation without relying on skill, effort, or passion.

3 Incompetent Executives

As much as I feel a kinship with the Smart-but-Stationary Manager, I feel in awe of the Incompetent Executive. They hold the secrets to your career success if you choose to accept them. It's easy to look down on Incompetent Executives, and I did for many years. But that's mostly jealousy talking and a lack of focus on what's most important to your career. The Incompetent Executive's unashamed pursuit of career success with little or no consideration for the conventional playbook is something to be studied rather than ridiculed. Since I started executing tactics from their game plan, my own career has taken off. Incompetent Executives come in various shapes and sizes but consistently exhibit characteristics from one of three classic profiles:

- ⤴ The Jack of All Trades.
- ⤴ Mr. Big Picture.
- ⤴ The Precision Passive Aggressive.

The Jack of All Trades

The first Incompetent Executive profile we'll examine is the Jack of All Trades. You will find one in every company. The Jack of All Trades is not to be confused with her Smart-but-Stationary cousin, the Go-to Guy. There are important differences between them. Recognizing them might make the difference between a promotion and a permanent vacation for you.

The Jack of All Trades is a generalist. Just good enough at everything to seem valuable, but not good enough at anything to be locked into a position. She is a magnet for promotions and impervious to layoffs. There is always a job for a Jack of All Trades, and the worse things get for a company, the more value she appears to have.

The Jack of All Trades thrives in periods of change and uncertainty. When the game gets messy, and the opportunities for advancement are ripe, the Jack of All Trades is at her best. She has just enough skill to make a superficial contribution to almost any role, which means the Jack of All Trades can capitalize on virtually every opportunity that arises. When everyone else is gossiping and griping about how the change will affect them, the Jack of All Trades is stepping up to the plate.

Granted, there is very little substance behind her work, but it doesn't matter. In my experience, it's 90 percent about attitude and 10 percent about ability when organizational change is afoot.

I've had the good fortune of working with several Jack of All Trades in my career. In fact, I spent a couple of years early in my career with the king—the "Jack of Spades," if you will. He is literally indestructible and yet to my mind has no particular management strengths whatsoever. As this manager gets moved around the organization to fill gaps and take on projects, he tends to make a quick positive impact, enough so the initial impression of his contribution is always positive. But then, once he's exceeded his depth, he proceeds to stop adding value altogether and, worse, he starts breaking things. But before real disaster hits, there is always some other job that needs his special attention. During the time I worked with this person, he literally ran marketing, IT, engineering, and support separately within a three-year period. Every time there was a vacancy, he was ready to step up to the plate. Then just as he was about to falter, the next opportunity presented itself. It's like career magic.

If you're asking yourself, *How do I become a Jack of All Trades?* it's all about developing a basic knowledge of everything, making your knowledge known with some well-placed criticisms when the timing is right, and being ready to pounce when opportunities present themselves. One very positive quality exhibited by nearly every Jack of All Trades I've known is self-confidence. They are always seeking new opportunities and chances for a big win. They're the business equivalent to a pinch hitter coming out in the bottom of the ninth inning. They truly believe they're going to hit a homerun, even if they have no reason to. Unfortunately, being a true Jack of All Trades is more an art form than a science, and takes many years and lonely nights with Google and Wikipedia to fine-tune. In the chapters to follow, we will examine a few key tactics they use that we can steal for our own game plans and that don't require decades of Web surfing to develop.

Mr. Big Picture

Our next Incompetent Executive is Mr. Big Picture. These managers live above the execution layer of the company in both mind and spirit. This is in stark contrast to the Task Master we saw earlier. It is the Incompetent Executive profile I'm personally drawn to the most and have incorporated into my game plan in a major way. Mr. Big Picture gets ahead in the company, not through expertise, but rather by conveying the underused and very powerful image of objectivity.

Mr. Big Picture ignores process and analytical minutia. He never gets emotionally involved with any project or idea; he's above that. This is the guy who starts and ends every discussion by relating the topic at hand back to the highest-level corporate objectives. And it doesn't matter how low level the subject is. You'll also never see him present an idea too passionately. He always comes equipped with options for consideration.

You might be thinking that this approach doesn't sound incompetent in the least; it just sounds like good business practice. Yes and no. Yes, it's a great business practice to adopt, although few people do it effectively. But the difference in this case is that Mr. Big Picture creates the illusion of objectivity to protect himself from the poor quality of his own work and ideas. This strategy is so powerful it literally provides insurance against ineptitude.

It goes like this: Mr. Big Picture has limited talent and he rarely has good ideas, but he knows it. Being the savvy fellow that he is, he has cultivated an image of objectivity, which means he always presents a variety of strategic alternatives. In presenting choices and by putting forth analysis on all sides, he is routinely commended for what looks to be thoughtful work. But in reality it's just camouflage for the fact that he actually has no idea what the right answer is.

Rather than make a call or stake a claim, Mr. Big Picture provides a decision-making framework for everyone else. It's a great way to handle difficult executive-level presentations and something I've incorporated into my personal playbook. Why bother assuming risk when you can win by simply moderating others to make the call for you? Then, when the idea succeeds, you are recognized for leading it. And if it fails, you are recognized for having provided all options objectively. It's a perpetual win-win for the Incompetent Executive. And it has no dependency whatsoever on talent or hard work.

In addition to his image of objectivity, you'll hear Mr. Big Picture referring to "the company" a lot more than most. It's an excellent way to avoid conflict and to deflect responsibility or ownership for a position. If an approach or idea is met with criticism, Mr. Big Picture doesn't defend directly but rather will say something like:

"As we know, the company is pushing for margins of 60 percent this year, which leaves us with several options. Option A has the benefit of control by lowering costs whereas Option B has the benefit of growth by expanding revenues. Both options are valid paths for us to take, and I can see pros and cons to both sides."

This is very much counter to how the Passion Player would respond, which would be more like:

> "I don't know how to make you understand that revenue expansion is the key to our success. I've worked through the numbers and haven't slept for a week. We must execute this strategy or we'll lose to the competition."

The Passion Player personalizes everything and communicates in absolutes and ultimatums; it's a far inferior strategy to Mr. Big Picture's objective approach if career advancement is the driving objective.

The Precision Passive Aggressive

Our final Incompetent Executive profile is the Precision Passive Aggressive. Not to be confused with your in-laws, these are the managers in your company who are truly wolves in sheep's clothing. Of all the Incompetent Executive profiles, Precision Passive Aggressives are the most difficult to spot because they operate in the shadows of the company and they always come bearing gifts. It's important to understand the difference between a normal, off-the-shelf passive aggressive person and a Precision Passive Aggressive manager. The former is just an annoyance to you. The latter is a real threat and someone playing to win.

The Precision Passive Aggressive succeeds in a company by creating an image of superiority over his or her peers. They accomplish this by purposefully seeking out opportunities to mentor their colleagues, whether they ask for mentorship or not. Like all Incompetent Executives, Precision

Passive Aggressives cannot rely on talent and performance as a career-advancement strategy because they are not skilled enough to contribute in this way. But they are driven. So they use another set of tactics to move up the ladder.

Precision Passive Aggressives avoid conflict as a rule. They work hard to build a reputation of benevolence within the company. They don't hold people accountable or drive them. Precision Passive Aggressives are publically supportive and always willing to help a colleague with a project or problem. But while this is the game being played out in the open, they play a sinister secondary game in the background.

Precision Passive Aggressives tactically work to build an image of superiority over the very same colleagues whom they purport to help. They find opportunities to let senior managers and executives know how they're mentoring their peers. This way they position themselves as more advanced and more prepared for promotion than the people they've helped. And very often, no help was ever requested in the first place. It's about image development for the Precision Passive Aggressive—an image designed to position them as leaders in the minds of the people who can influence their upward mobility.

I had the opportunity to work at a company several years ago where I was surrounded by Precision Passive Aggressives. It was as though there was a sign on the front door welcoming them into the company. One of the big warning signs that you are prey for a Precision Passive Aggressive is when they start inviting themselves to your meetings to "help out" or "stay on the same page—ostensibly to contribute, but in reality to take credit and marginalize your success in a highly visible project. It was not uncommon for a meeting that started out with five people on the invite list to balloon to 12 or more by the time it started. Precision Passive Aggressives are like vultures to a dying wildebeest, and this company was the Kalahari Game Reserve.

So next time someone offers to help you review your work, or help bring your project back on track, think before blindly accepting the offer. It's rare people want to take on incremental work for no clear gain. It may be more likely the do-gooder in question is looking for an opportunity to let people know how he saved the day and position himself above you in the perceptions of your superiors.

How does one become a Precision Passive Aggressive? You don't. Remember: Incompetent Executives are not perfect corporate specimens, and the Precision Passive Aggressive in particular has many flaws. What we will do in the chapters to come is hand pick the best parts of the profile, steal them for own arsenals, and leave the rest behind.

━━━━━

In the final section, we'll look at three Lost Souls. There is nothing in these profiles for us to emulate but it's important to recognize the behaviors we want to avoid at all costs. Lost Souls exhibit them in spades.

3 Lost Souls

It's important to call out a few other profiles you'll see around your company that can often be confused for the Incompetent Executive or the Smart-but-Stationary Manager. Whereas I have admiration and hope for both of these groups, the final group, the Lost Souls, I'm afraid is unsalvageable. Lost Souls are totally unaware that a career game is even being contested. This role requires a special lack of self-awareness, which precludes you from ever advancing your career in a meaningful way.

Can a Lost Soul become an Incompetent Executive? Probably not. Lost Souls lack the tactical abilities and savvy necessary to overcome their limited talent and get ahead. Can a Lost Soul become a Smart-but-Stationary Manager? Definitely not. You simply can't create raw talent and intelligence out of nothing.

But before we get ahead of ourselves, let me point out that you will at times see flashes of the Lost Soul in yourself. But these will be your mistakes, not your standard. So if you've dabbled in some Lost Soulness in your time, it's no big deal. You can overcome that. But if any of what follows describes you to a T, I'm afraid you are truly lost.

Let's profile the most common Lost Souls to get a better understanding of why they are so fatally flawed. There are three types worth talking about:

- ⊃ The Social Chair.
- ⊃ The Gossip Girl/Guy.
- ⊃ The No-Change Agent.

The Social Chair

The Social Chair in your department bears a striking resemblance to your high school student council president or pep squad leader, or whoever it was that planned your senior prom. I suspect they arrange more than their fair share of picnics and probably play Ultimate Frisbee. Evidently this group missed the memo between high school and Silicon Valley that the game had changed. They continue to try and score career points by organizing company activities. They haven't realized that nobody else is assigning any real value to this stuff.

The Social Chair cannot get ahead in a company for two reasons. First, organizing social events creates a perception of subservience in the minds of others. As much as this sounds callous, you must be creating an image of leadership—not as a coordinator—to be taken seriously as a future executive. And although executives at your company may laud you for being so helpful, they're never going to promote you for it. The second reason is a matter of priorities. If you are concentrating time and energy organizing events, you are not using it to actively manage your career. There simply aren't enough hours in the day to do both.

But what about corporate culture, you may ask? Isn't there value in building that?

Honestly no, not in this way. Real corporate culture has very little to do with activities and events. It's about fairness and opportunity, transparency and trust. When the time comes for reconciliation—at promotion or layoff time, social contributions are at best pointed to as the unfortunate downside of having to let a nice person go.

It's very uncommon to see a Social Chair evolve into anything beyond a mid-level manager. Am I saying you should never participate in company social events and become a grumpy old stick in the mud? No, not at all. Let me be clear, I'm saying do not be the person who organizes these things. You have to attend social events at work because it's a great chance to network up the corporate ladder. But just make sure you're on the right side of the lemonade stand at the company picnic.

The Gossip Girl/Guy

The Gossip Girl is a bit of a special case for Lost Souls in that I've actually seen a few turn it around and become successful. However, to do so usually requires a role change or a new workplace entirely.

This group operates and thrives only at its own level of the organization and below. They roam around the herd of low-level managers and staff, talking and gossiping and griping about senior management. They always seem to be complaining about something. And because they rarely get ahead in the company, it fuels a self-perpetuating cycle of gripe.

Look around your company and point out the group of friends who always sit together, go to events together, and always seem to be commiserating about something. These are the Gossip Guys. They're in every company and you may have fallen into the gossip trap a few times yourself. It's quite natural to want to gripe and gossip. It feels good to relate with people experiencing the same feelings as you. It's also a losing career strategy.

One of the most important pieces of advice I give my friends and clients is to never gossip at work under any circumstance. It's a classic example of a zero-upside proposition. What I mean by that is gossiping and griping with your peers about upper management can never actually win you anything. It only makes you feel a sense of temporary emotional satisfaction. But what it can do is crush your career when people see you doing it. Gossiping and griping at work is akin to playing a hand of blackjack where if you win, you keep your original bet, but if you lose the house takes all your money, your house, and your car. Your best case is neutral. Your worst case is devastating.

There's nothing to be gained whatsoever from being a Gossip Girl because the people you're bonding with cannot help you advance in your career and the people you're griping about have all the power over your success or failure. Do not fall into the gossip trap.

The No-Change Agent

No-Change Agents are true creatures of habit. These individuals are held together by routines and processes as though they're the very oxygen that fuels them at work. Typically they've been in the same job for a long time. They walk around with project plans and process documents, seemingly more concerned for "how" initiatives get executed than "why" or "to what end."

No-Change Agents normally exist quite peacefully for a while until something big happens: a company restructuring, an acquisition, a new strategy, role changes, new management. Change, as you might imagine, is kryptonite for No-Change Agents. They simply cannot function in a fluctuating, uncertain work environment. This is the biggest reason No-Change Agents don't get ahead. In my experience, periods of change are the best possible opportunities for career upward mobility, and this is when No-Change Agents are at their absolute worst.

Acquisitions and other disruptive corporate changes are times of mass confusion. People get laid off, roles change, new processes and systems and strategies are introduced. It's a total mess and many people, especially No-Change Agents, cannot handle that kind of uncertainty. Rather than tactically harvest these periods for opportunities, the No-Change Agent fights against the change. But this is like fighting against a rip

33333333

tide—the force of change is too powerful. All you can succeed in doing by fighting inevitable change is tiring yourself out and ultimately drowning.

You've probably seen No-Change Agents at your workplace. You may have been tempted to behave this way yourself from time to time. They come into work after a change with a bad attitude and proceed to up the gossip and griping by a factor of 10. They constantly grumble in meetings and harp on about why the new way isn't aligned with "the way we've always done things." No-Change Agents become fixated on preserving the old culture and brand. They constantly talk about ways to return to how things used to operate. Do not spend time with these people, and under no circumstance act like this yourself.

To be successful in your career, you need to be on the winning side of change more often than not. The Incompetent Executive is a master at this. Because No-Change Agents are at their worst when the opportunities for success are at their greatest, they will always come out on the losing side of the career game.

Unlike the Smart-but-Stationary Manager and the Incompetent Executive, if you find yourself in the Lost Soul profiles, you're in deep trouble. I won't sugarcoat it. On the upside, the mere fact you're reading this book suggests that you're conscious of the need to actively manage your career and therefore you're likely not dominated by these attributes. It's okay if you've dabbled in gossip or you've been known to organize a team outing now and again. But if this is what defines your career strategy, you have a long way to go.

Examples, Please

Now that we've studied the players in the game, we're ready for the next step. In the next chapter, we'll walk through some real-life examples from my own career. I've used fictitious companies and names, but the scenarios are real. We'll see how different people handle common career situations. We'll witness firsthand how the Incompetent Executive almost always comes out on top.

This is where we'll start stealing the best tactics the Incompetent Executive employs for our own game plans. The key is to not become an Incompetent Executive yourself, but rather to take from the best of them and leave the worst behind. The combination of your intellect and talent with their tactics will make you a force to be reckoned with for the rest of your career.

Chapter 4

Your Playbook: 7 Lessons to Steal the Corner Office

We now understand the environment we're playing in, the right mindset to have, and the competitors we face. It's time to start building a playbook to really move your career in the right direction.

During the past 10 years, I've systematically tested all the tactics of the Incompetent Executive. I've studied and practiced the dark arts that make them successful in spite of their inherent flaws. Through my own trial and error, I've hand-picked the top seven lessons you can put into your arsenal tomorrow to kick start your career.

In each of the next seven sections, we'll cover a key lesson stolen from the playbook of the Incompetent Executive. For each strategy, I'll recount two stories: The first will be a story of how I or one of my Smart-but-Stationary colleagues dealt with a business scenario incorrectly. We'll do some analysis on where mistakes were made and how to avoid them. The second will be a story of how an Incompetent Executive from my past handled a similar scenario. We'll see how they come out on top despite their classical limitations as managers. At the end of each lesson, I'll summarize the most important tactics and give you a clear playbook for how to incorporate it into your day-to-day routine.

Let's get started.

1. Never Be Passionate About Your Ideas

In this section, we're going to hear the stories of Victor and Otto. These tales are near and dear to my heart. Victor's story comes from one of my first experiences as a product manager. Otto's story comes from a recent experience I witnessed from the sidelines. They illustrate a mistake most often made by Passion Players and other highly talented but inexperienced managers. More importantly, they will teach us a valuable tactic for advancing our careers. We'll see how cultivating an image of objectivity is often more powerful than conveying an image of passion—powerful enough that when applied even by an incompetent manager, it can compensate for a lack of subject matter expertise and adequate preparation. We'll learn how even the most talented of us can fall into a dangerous trap if we focus too much on evangelizing our ideas and not enough on tactically advancing our careers.

The Tale of Victor the Visionary

As he shut down his iPad, Victor slowly let the air escape from his lungs, as though he'd just witnessed something truly amazing. Having just binge-watched 10 of his favorite TED talks, he felt ready for the day that lay ahead. Victor had a certain sense of clarity that only came around once in a while.

And he felt it now in a major way. He had finally figured out what had been missing from the company's product strategy, and he knew exactly what they had to do.

New Jobs

Victor flipped carefully through the presentation he'd spent all night building. *I'm going to transform this company and revolutionize the industry as we know it,* he breathed, as though he was opening the lid to the Ark of the Covenant. Certainly these slides held the secrets to success for BiggieNet Ltd. Granted, he had only been with the company for a few months as a junior associate product manager, but he felt like he had earned the respect of the team already. More importantly, his vision was the right one. *They'll listen to me,* he thought. *I'll make them listen.*

Victor was not one to delay. And so, late that night he sent a meeting invitation to all the senior product staff with the subject "Project X—Our Next Generation Strategy." He would unveil his vision first thing the next morning. *They're going to be so excited when they hear my strategy,* he promised himself before settling in for his typical night of tossing and turning.

"This oughtta be good," Jenna said sarcastically to George, her senior product manager and right-hand man. As the head of product management, Jenna, along with the rest of the team, had received Victor's late-night invitation. She and George had made a point of getting to the meeting room a little early to chat about what they were likely to see. Jenna had been around the block a few times, and she'd seen more than her fair share of ambitious young product managers. *I was one once,* she recalled with a tinge of regret. Every one of them wanted to be the next Steve Jobs, and so Jenna carried a healthy dose of skepticism around with her wherever she went.

"Come on, now; give him a chance," George counseled. "Who knows? Maybe it'll actually be good." Of course, he didn't believe what he was saying, but he'd also been around enough himself to know Jenna had a tendency to be a bit territorial when it came to the strategy for the product. More than one product manager had been cut down by her. Including him.

Two TEDS Are Better Than One

Before George and Jenna could get into it any further, the rest of the product team entered the room and took their seats. Conspicuous by his absence, Victor had not officially entered the room, but he had projected a slide on the wall displaying only *Project X.* He had used some type of slide animation to make the font of the "X" pulse like a beating heart. *I hope that heartbeat animation wasn't too much,* he second-guessed himself for a millisecond before quickly snapping back to his usual optimism. Victor steadied himself and marched into the room with purpose.

"Good morning, gang," he powered out with arms wide open.

"Hey, Victor," a couple of them said, clearly not sharing in the magnitude of the moment.

Rather than speak right away, Victor held a blank stare, fixed at an imaginary point in the heavens as though he was connecting to the source of his divine inspiration. Because he was so focused on his TED-like presentation skills, Victor missed the quick eye-roll exchange between Jenna and George, who had a lot of other things to do that morning.

Victor finally began.

The presentation seemed to start almost at the beginning of time in a grand effort to set context for his strategy. The images of Neanderthals evolving into modern humans as a metaphor for his strategy amused his cynical manager. *Oh, no, you didn't. You used the cavemen,* Jenna shook her head almost imperceptibly.

After much preface and preamble about the evolution of the modern consumer, Victor finally pitched his strategy with all the enthusiasm and awe he could deliver.

Nailed it, he told himself immediately upon completion.

"Thank you, Victor," Jenna expressed quite sincerely. "That was a thoughtful presentation, and I think there may be a few things in there for us to consider," she said honestly but without much fanfare. As painful as it was to admit, it wasn't the worst idea she'd ever heard—Toastmasters speech aside. Had they left it at that point, Jenna may have even embraced aspects of the strategy, as it was not without merit. But for Victor, her curt reaction felt like a slap in the face. He just couldn't contain himself.

"I don't understand!" Victor reacted in front of the entire group. "Shouldn't we take some time to lay out an implementation plan? If we don't move on this right away, the competition will get there before us. We have so much to do to get this launched!" He was pleading for support.

"Easy, tiger," Jenna scolded calmly, as though she was mostly ignoring him anyway. "There was some good stuff in there but we're not going to move the entire product strategy just like that. Why don't you set up a second meeting with the team 30 days from now? That will give us some time to noodle the ideas."

"30 days?!" Victor yelped in a jolt reaction. "Okay, okay. I'll set it up," he managed to eke out as he forced himself to gain control.

Twenty minutes later, Victor replayed the meeting in his head while he opened one of the many cans of baked beans he kept in his desk drawer. He couldn't help but work himself back into a frenzy. Jenna was just jealous. He was sure of it. *She's been here five years and she's never come up with anything like my vision. And the rest of them are just cattle. They wouldn't know a product strategy if it hit them in the face.*

Crimes of Passion

As he ate his beans straight from the can, Victor played a thousand scenarios in his head. He had to push this through. He owed it to the company. They simply didn't have time to wait or the competition would beat them to the punch. *If I have to leave a few bodies on the side of the road, then so be it,* he told himself. He had to think of something. Maybe he should march straight into the CEO's office and deliver the company-saving strategy on a silver platter. He'd ride triumphantly off into the sunset, high-fiving Mark Zuckerberg along the way. But it wasn't time for that yet.

In all likelihood, Victor could still have salvaged things at this point. He might have even been able to advance his strategy in the long run. In fact, later that same day, Jenna had remarked to one of the members of the team that Victor had made a few strong points she needed to consider for the next release of the product. But when Victor learned of this, it only riled him up further.

"It's a strategy," he patronized to anyone who would listen. "You can't pick and choose the pieces you want!" He was offended.

Victor was determined. He was certainly not going to let a couple of hiccups get in the way of his master strategy. How could he? This was going to be his legacy. So Victor continued to campaign day after day, using every backchannel he could think of to bring his colleagues onside. Maybe if he could create a groundswell of support, he could sway Jenna onto his side. But what happened instead was a lesson that would take Victor many years to fully understand and many more to fully recover from.

Thirty days had passed, and it was time to pick up the discussion about Victor's product strategy. Although it was only the second formal meeting, Victor, of course, had been a busy boy all month. In fact, he'd made a point of holding several impromptu meetings with members of the team. He had been seen cornering innocent passersby as they walked down the hall to bring them onboard. Victor's typical conversation went something like, "Jenna just doesn't get it but I know you do. If we don't move fast on this, we'll miss the opportunity...." Yet even with all of this distraction and insubordination, Jenna remained patient. After all, Victor had talent; nobody would argue that. But then he went too far.

The morning prior to meeting day, Victor drove himself to the brink anticipating Jenna's likely position. *I have to make her understand. I owe it to the company to make them aware of this.* He just couldn't leave things to chance. It was too important. And so he justified his next move. Just like in the thousand scenarios he'd played out in his head, Victor marched upstairs into the CEO's office and pitched his strategy. But this time, it didn't go quite as he'd imagined in his daydreams.

The meeting itself was short and not particularly alarming from Victor's perspective. Not at first, at least. The CEO had not had a lot of time to talk but he listened to a condensed version of the pitch. When it was over, he shook Victor's hand, thanked him for his time, and then said one final thing: "I trust you shared this with Jenna before coming to me," said more as a statement than a question.

"Umm, well, of course." Victor told a white lie as they parted company.

Checkmate. Victor fist bumped himself as he walked back to his cubicle to prepare for the second strategy meeting. The CEO had shown a lot of interest. Jenna would have to listen to him now.

Passion Penalty

It was meeting day, which meant Victor went through his standard pre-game ritual. He watched his TED talks, put on his black turtleneck and jeans, and headed to the office in the brand new Tesla Electric Roadster he'd borrowed money from his parents to lease. With the CEO seemingly onside, he felt confident that convincing Jenna would be much easier now.

Victor walked into the meeting room ready for anything. But before he could get set up, Jenna walked in and asked him to sit down.

"Victor," she said calmly as though she were a grade-school teacher about to gently scold a child. "We've decided to make a change."

"Okay," Victor stared back blankly as he tried to figure out how bad things were about to get.

"I had an interesting chat with our CEO yesterday afternoon. He was quite impressed by some of your ideas. But like me, he has major concerns about your attitude and insubordination." She paused briefly.

"But!" Victor started for a nanosecond.

She delivered her next message as though any opposition by Victor would lead to him carrying a box out of the building: "We've decided to move you into a new role as special projects associate. We think this will give you a chance to use all your great skills and also work on some of your areas for improvement."

A range of emotions ran through Victor as he took in the news. He may have been young, but he knew that "special projects associate" was one step from the door. They had probably given careful consideration to letting him go.

"Okay, Jenna," he stumbled. "I understand."

He managed to summon enough resolve to handle himself professionally for the remainder of the short meeting. Victor, after all, was an intelligent guy. He'd just let his passion and ambition cloud his judgment. He promised himself there and then he'd never make this mistake again.

What We Can Learn From Victor

Victor's story is proof that not all passion is positive in a corporate environment and that talent without tact can be deadly to your career. Though you may think Victor's missteps were obvious and a little over the top, I assure you I see these antics play out all the time, and I personally acted this way in the early part of my career. In fact, I see these behaviors more often now than I did a decade ago, as the business and consumer world have begun to iconize the great visionaries and innovators.

For many intelligent managers, the idea of being recognized as a strategist and innovator is the driving force for them on a day-to-day basis. Although this is not always a career-limiting move, it can be if we're not careful. Ultimately, the success or failure of playing this strategy depends more on how you deliver innovation and less on the innovation itself. Victor let his passion and hubris get in the way of an effective career game plan, and it nearly cost him his job. He lost sight of the most important career objective and confused being right with being effective.

I want to be clear: I'm not advocating against innovation or being strategically minded. Obviously these are great qualities in a manager and much needed in every organization. But there is a right way and a wrong way to pursue innovation in a corporate environment. Victor clearly chose the wrong approach. If you look back on your own career I'm sure you can point to a few Victors, some of whom grew to be corporate rock stars and others who likely became early exits from the organization. Victor nearly paid the ultimate price because he played his strategy incorrectly. His fate had absolutely nothing to do with his intellect.

Real power, and, ultimately real career success, come more from endearing people than from convincing them of anything. You need your colleagues to want you to be successful. In my experience, when you care too much about an idea, you inevitably end up having to make certain sacrifices to push it through. More often than not, the first sacrifice is your objectivity, which is an image all managers should strive to convey. The second sacrifice is relationship capital that you will need at some point to influence your career advancement.

But wait—what could be more endearing than true passion? Isn't passion what will make people want to follow you? That is only partially correct. Passion for the best path, irrespective of whose idea it was, is a virtue that endears people. Passion for *your* path, because you *know* it to be right, is just a bullying tactic disguised as innovativeness. If you want to be a true visionary and motivate people, you need to demonstrate a passion for what's best irrespective of what that might mean for you personally.

With Victor it was all about "his" idea, "my" strategy. And though he may have presented some analysis, he never allowed the key influencers in the company to perform their own diligence. He chose to force his ideas on his colleagues rather than present all possible ideas and allow the right one to win on its own merits.

———————

Now let's take a look at the story of Otto the Objective to see how an Incompetent Executive approaches a similar scenario so we can steal a few of his strategies for our own game plan.

The Tale of Otto the Objective

"So I like kittens! Sue me!" he barked at his computer screen and slammed the keyboard. Otto exited the forum he was arguing back and forth in. *I loathe dog people,* he thought to himself and took a deep breath. Otto looked around his home office, pausing a couple of times to smile a one of the many pictures of his favorite cat, Bugsy. It helped him to relax. Internet trolls drove him crazy. If it weren't for Bugsy he'd have long ago gone over the edge. Otto loved cats more than anything. They were his great joy in life, and for as long as he could remember, he dreamed of the day he could leave his job at K-Tech Inc. and start his own feline grooming service.

"It's more like a day spa for very discerning kitties," he explained to his doting mother, who tidied up around him. It was his dream, but sadly just that—a dream. As a 35-year-old man, Otto realized that for the foreseeable future, he needed to stay in his current job as a pricing manager for K-Tech. He had to pay the bills and save up for the day he would quit to launch his dream business.

Purrrricing Strategy

Otto never told anyone at the office about his entrepreneurial dreams. They probably wouldn't understand anyway. That said, he was pretty sure his colleagues sensed his heart wasn't in pricing management. Pricing didn't exactly come naturally to Otto. He found he spent a disproportionate amount of time trying to convince people he understood pricing strategy, and less time actually implementing models and policies. But Otto managed to get by using his very cat-like tactical sensibility.

Perhaps it was from so many years of covering up his short-comings, but Otto, more than most, understood how to work with people.

Otto had a very unique approach to managing projects and solving business problems. When he was assigned a big project like the one he worked on presently, Otto tried not to get caught up in deciphering the optimal solution. He focused on his "foolproof framework" instead. It was an approach he'd used for several years that made it much easier to get things done. To his credit, Otto understood where his strengths and weaknesses lay. He had learned this the hard way early on in his career. Otto recognized that it was often more effective to help people come up with the answer themselves than figuring it out yourself and then convincing others you're right. This was especially true for Otto, who frankly had very few bright ideas as they pertained to pricing. He reserved that kind of thinking for his own business plans.

Otto was tasked with building and implementing a new pricing strategy to adjust to changes in how customers were starting to buy their line of Internet security solutions. Increasingly, K-Tech customers wanted to pay for products and services on a monthly basis rather than in an upfront capital expense. This certainly made sense to Otto, as many of his personal expenses like Web hosting, e-mail, and other services were now priced this way. But as simple as it all sounded on the surface, it didn't take long for Otto to realize he was out of his depth.

"Subscriptions, leasing, perpetual licensing, financing, site licenses," he rambled to his mom. "I can't keep track of it all and God knows I'll never be able to figure out what's best for us," he concluded with obvious frustration in his voice.

"I believe in you, Otto," his mom said with a comforting pat on the back.

"Honestly, Mom, I just don't know this time." But just before let himself get too carried away, Otto regained his feline composure and resolved to do what he always did in these situations.

Foolproof Feline

This calls for my world famous "foolproof framework," Otto thought to himself as he tried to summon some emotional momentum. He started drawing two columns on a piece of paper. He'd done this four other times, and it always seemed to work. Otto sometimes worried people would see through his approach and call him out for being a fraud, but he had no other choice and pressed on.

Otto proceeded to build a very straightforward decision-making framework that outlined *all* the possible options for the company. It had a list of the pros and cons for each without any bias one way or the other. Of course, Otto had no idea what the right answer was, so it was impossible for him to bias the decision-making process anyhow. He did his best to be thorough in his list of options and added a quick situational overview to provide some context for the would-be decision-makers.

"I wish I could take you guys with me," Otto purred to his favorite kitties while they gobbled up their individually pre-pared breakfasts on the morning of his big presentation.

Even though he had no love for his job, Otto was still a little nervous about the meeting that would take place in a couple of hours. There was no question the executives expected a formal proposal and he simply did not have one to deliver. Otto had no idea what the right pricing approach was, and frankly, he didn't care all that much. So he carried a healthy dose of anxiety as he kissed each kitten goodbye and left for the office.

The meeting room was full. More than 10 K-Tech managers from various departments anxiously awaited the pricing discussion set to take place. There was a healthy dose of skepticism in the air, as was normal for a dialogue on such an important and complex subject. It was apparent even before the meeting began that everyone had brought an opinion with them.

"If he says one word about leasing, I'm walking out that door," grumbled Dawson, who ran the product team, as he watched Otto struggle with the projector, wearing what appeared to be a Hello Kitty sweatshirt.

"I'm more worried about the international rollout. I guarantee you he hasn't planned for foreign exchange," Chris, the VP of international sales, added as the audience seemed to collectively warm up for what most expected to be a highly contentious meeting.

Very aware of the high stakes, Otto finally got the presentation to project on the screen, albeit with a heavy dose of fumbling around. He felt nervous but optimistic. He was strangely comforted by the fact he had no horse in the race. He could honestly say he didn't care what the eventual outcome was so long as he came out on top.

Nothing can go wrong while I'm wearing my lucky shirt, Otto reassured himself, only half believing it. And then he began.

"Good morning, guys." Otto greeted the group trying his best to look like a pricing expert.

"Good morning," some of the group responded with eyes that seemed to dare Otto to make a mistake.

"I know pricing is a hot issue for us right now and each of you has strong opinions on the best path forward. I am sure many of you have very valid concerns to share. In light of that, I felt the most prudent approach for this meeting would be to walk you through a framework to evaluate our options collaboratively. If we follow it together, we will all be heard and we can objectively weigh all alternatives available to us."

I hope they bought that, Otto thought to himself. *I'm going to need all the help I can get.*

For the better part of the next hour, Otto guided the team through an evaluation of every possible pricing strategy under the sun, a few of which didn't totally make sense given the strategic context. But nobody seemed to call much attention to that. The meeting, as anticipated, was very heated. For most of it Otto wished he were somewhere else entirely. There were debates and arguments and a few angry moments. But not once was any of the anger directed at Otto. The VP of sales argued with the product manager. The distribution manager argued with the retailing manager. The only person seemingly without a target on his back was Otto. He was completely out of the line of fire. He found a few key opportunities to bring the group back on point and encourage them to look at the issues objectively—and they seemed to respond.

When the meeting was over, the team had reached consensus on many of the issues. They'd aligned on a subscription pricing model as the optimal strategy for the company. There were still several execution details to work out, but the heavy lifting was done. Otto could handle the small stuff without a problem.

"Great meeting, Otto," a couple of them said as they left.

"Well done, pricing guru," the VP of sales complimented sincerely as he went to his next meeting.

The meeting had been a success. They had found a strategy that they could align with, and Otto was no worse for wear.

Chalk up another victory to Team Kitty, he giggled to himself as he closed the meeting room door.

Your Personal Playbook: Never Be Passionate About Your Ideas

We learned an important lesson from the stories of Victor and Otto. It's easy for talented, creative managers to fall into the trap of favoring passion over objectivity. More often than not, our ideas actually are good, and it can be extremely frustrating when the corporation is slow or reluctant to adopt them. The key for us to remember is that ideas alone will not get you ahead. A career strategy based on passionate pursuits is too high risk. It may pay off occasionally, but it's not necessary to achieve success. Here are a few guidelines you can use to develop the extremely powerful image of objectivity. Incorporate them into your game plan and they'll never let you down.

- Always present options. Even if you're convinced you know the correct strategy, you must always present alternative courses of action. We're taught to do this in business school, but you rarely see it executed effectively in a high-paced corporate setting.

- Don't present fake options. Presenting bogus options in hopes of stacking the deck in favor of your idea is a rookie move. If you can't think of other strategic options to present, you are probably overly passionate about your own concept. People can see through fake options, and it only makes you look immature.

- Learn to embrace any decision. It takes maturity to embrace options you don't personally favor. But in the career game, that kind of objective, professional approach will win you way more points than any one big idea you may have. Be prepared to enthusiastically embrace whatever strategic path the most influential people ultimately align with.

2. Embrace the Changes Everyone Else Hates

In this section, we're going to hear the stories of Nancy and Carl. Identical scenarios play out in companies on a daily basis. Nancy's tale comes from an experience I had working for a startup software company. It illustrates a very common mistake managers make during periods of transition and uncertainty. Carl's story comes from the same experience, albeit from the perspective of another manager I knew who handled the change strategically. We'll see great examples of why you need to prepare a tactical game plan when organizational change is afoot. Let's take a look at how two managers handled the same situation differently, and how their tactics, not their competence, determined their fates.

The Tale of No-Change Nancy

Process Makes Perfect! She should have had t-shirts made up with that slogan. Nancy was giggling to herself as she reflected on all the hard work she'd put in the past three years. Granted, it had been like pulling teeth at times, but as she looked back on the progress EastStar Inc. had made, and her part in it, Nancy couldn't help but feel proud of her accomplishments.

It had been a long road. Though Nancy had initially wondered if she was cut out for the startup culture, she had proven, to herself at least, that she had what it took to succeed. It was a bonus that along the way she had given them exactly what they needed. *A little process goes a long way.*

A Creature of Habit

Nancy was a creature of habit and ritual. Yes, more than once she'd been accused of being a bit too focused on the minutia, maybe even a little rigid in her approach. But she knew in her heart that consistent process and procedure were the lifeblood and safety net of every great company.

Before she had accepted the role at EastStar Inc., Nancy cut her teeth for the better part of a decade with one of the world's largest manufacturing companies. Her boss and mentor had drilled into her, day after day, the importance of process and process governance. Nancy was a natural.

There is something comforting in knowing you're truly great at what you do, she daydreamed that morning. Whenever a new system was deployed or a new operational process needed to get rolled out, they called on Nancy. *I'm the princess of process,* she blushed, as she got carried away with her own giddiness.

Nancy had every reason to be excited and proud. She had become a fixture at EastStar, and although she occasionally rubbed a few people the wrong way, she had the engineering team running like a well-oiled machine. Nancy was okay with ruffling a few feathers. *That's the price of process!* She could almost hear her old mentor barking over their afternoon Americanos.

EastStar IPO?

Today is going to be a great day. Nancy's giddiness started to resurface. The company had been planning its initial public offering (IPO) for a long time, and after what seemed like an endless series of delays and missteps it looked like it must finally be here. Everyone in the company had received the same e-mail from the CEO last night. There was to be a company all-hands meeting the following morning. *This can only mean one thing,* she thought.

In honor of the big day, she decided to have a little fun with her outfit. It was a game they liked to play on her team. So, as she put on her vintage Salt & Peppa concert t-shirt, Nancy couldn't help herself but to giggle one last time at the irony of the initials on her t-shirt and wondered how long it would take the others to get the joke.

Nancy completed her morning pre-work checklist and arrived at the office a good 15 minutes early, as was her standard. She was never late, and that went for projects, appointments, and everything else. People respected her for it too. As she popped out of her beloved Chrysler PT Cruiser, Nancy could see her colleagues gathering out front, no doubt buzzing on what was about to happen.

"I bet we're going at $12.30 a share!" she heard one of the more senior engineers say, as he seemingly did the mental mathematics on how much he stood to make on the IPO.

"That's conservative. I've heard 6x and 7x multiples could be in play. I'd venture $15.00 is possible," one of the software architects said rather optimistically. It seemed like everyone had an opinion.

Unlike many of her colleagues, Nancy didn't spend time thinking about IPO valuations and stock prices. To her credit, Nancy understood there would be blackout periods and that market forces would ultimately determine the value of the company over the months to come. There was a lot to play out still. In fact, she had noted recently that one of the other companies in their industry, GenCloud, had gone public, and the highly touted stock had plummeted shortly after the offering.

From Nancy's perspective, it was not really about the money anyway. For one thing, Nancy had only been with the company three years, so she didn't have quite as many stock options as the other managers. Mostly she was just excited to work for a public company again, where process and procedure were more important, and where she would be valued even more.

Everyone filed into the auditorium like children on the first day of school. U2's "It's a Beautiful Day" pounded on the speakers to everyone's delight. "Cheesiness aside, that was a nice touch," Nancy quipped to one of her colleagues as they took their seats. When the music faded and the company's CEO took the podium, Nancy and a few others couldn't help but notice the group of five other men and women behind him whom they'd never seen before.

"Must be the investment bankers," an accounts receivable clerk to her left whispered and nodded at the same time.

The room got quiet and the CEO, with a huge smile on his face, began to speak.

"Good morning, team!" he belted.

"Good morning!" the audience roared back.

"I'm so happy to be standing in front of you today to deliver the great news so many of us have been waiting for." He continued, "As many of you know, the capital markets have been a little challenging lately. We've had our share of difficult decisions to make as we try to secure the right path forward to take our company to the next level."

Nancy's stomach sunk just a little as that last comment lingered. She leaned in a little closer as if trying to be the first one to hear what the CEO would say next.

"You all know about GenCloud's struggles with their IPO, and we don't want to go down like that," he shouted defiantly. "So the board and the investors and I have made a decision that will benefit us all and fuel our company for the next decade and more."

Nancy swallowed deliberately. He finally laid it out: "And so, without any further ado, I'm thrilled to introduce you to our new partner, LaserNet Global!"

It took about 10 seconds to register for Nancy. The audience, feeling similarly confused, half clapped as they seemed to be working through it at the same time she was. Questions rushed through Nancy's head: *Partner? What does that mean? LaserNet? I haven't heard that name in 10 years. What about the IPO?* But before Nancy could send herself into a total meltdown, the CEO began to lay out the details for the group.

"I know for many of you this will seem like a bit of a change in course," he said with hands up and palms facing the crowd as if assuming a defensive guard. "But I can assure you we should all be excited to be joining the LaserNet team! And with that I'm so happy to introduce you to our new friends...."

The Aftermath

The 30 minutes that followed were a total blur for Nancy and almost everyone else in the room as well. It's not that an acquisition was a total surprise. It kind of made sense with the public markets being so unpredictable recently. But Laser-Net? Anyone but LaserNet! They were well-known for being an aging dinosaur that hadn't seriously been a player for the better part of a decade. It seemed more like a path to the grave than a path to the future.

With a great deal of concern, Nancy spent the rest of the day doing what she did best. She made a list of all the questions she had and resolved not to let anything or any company get in the way of the progress they were making. *I can make this work. I know I can,* Nancy lied to herself.

Over the course of the next four weeks, Nancy's mood ran the gamut from shock, to optimism, to concern, and now to plain old anger. There had been endless speeches and company events with the LaserNet executives. They assured their new EastStar colleagues that they'd acquired the company for its innovation *and* its personnel. This would not be one of those acquisitions where they rip and replace all the great people and processes.

"Hands off," they seemed to recite all the time with big smiles and the best of intentions. "That's what we've been told to do and we intend to do just that. We're so excited you've joined the LaserNet family." Unfortunately, it didn't take more than a couple of weeks for Nancy to see the first indications that this might not be the case.

The New Regime

The first episode Nancy could recall took place at the joint sales kickoff meeting. All the operations and sales managers assembled to present their quarterly plans. This kickoff would be uniquely complicated as they sought to merge the two teams together with a variety of different people and processes. There seemed to be a great deal of tension in the air; it felt more like an audition than a business meeting.

Nancy had prepared her plan as she always did: meticulously. It was the result of more than a year of work and she was determined to wow everyone. Her presentation focused on a rollout plan for the latest phase of her retail sales process. Six weeks earlier, it would have gone off without a hitch. But things had changed.

The first few presentations went off without contention—mostly polite nods and withheld questions as the two camps were feeling each other out. When it was Nancy's turn to present, she started with her usual confident and matter-of-fact approach. But she was a mere two minutes in when she was stopped dead in her tracks.

"I'm sorry, Nancy, but that's not how we do it at Laser-Net," said a smiling face in the middle of the room.

Nancy let that one slide and acted courteous in her response. But it didn't stop there. It seemed every time she presented an idea or process, they said the same thing.

That's not the LaserNet way! Nancy mocked to herself later with a fake smiley face on.

It wasn't until she presented the crown jewel in her process portfolio that Nancy finally lost it. She had worked on a partner sales registration process for the better part of two years and it was flawless. What's more, Nancy had spent countless hours teaching and re-teaching the EastStar sales team and distribution partners how to follow it. So this time when she heard "that's not the LaserNet way," Nancy fired back with a vengeance.

"Well, it might not be the LaserNet way," she said with poison on her tongue, "but it's damn sure the right way!"

That didn't go well, Nancy thought to herself later as she recalled the condescending looks on their faces. The LaserNet managers had proceeded to simultaneously pacify and patronize her as they explained why their tried and true processes were best. Whereas Nancy's process might work well for a small company, it just couldn't scale. It had not been pretty.

Push Comes to Shove

After the kickoff meeting, it all changed for Nancy. She had tried to be courteous. She walked people through her processes. She was happy to educate anyone willing to listen. But it seemed like nobody cared to understand, no matter how friendly they seemed on the outside. Nancy vowed, right there and then, she wouldn't go down without a fight. It was her nature to be persistent; you needed to be in process operations, and it had served her well in the past. So she dug her heals in and set her mind on showing them the light. Whenever she had the chance, Nancy was determined to show people why the EastStar process was the right one for the future.

Nancy started by trying to rally support from her colleagues. "This is why LaserNet is losing in the market," she said to anyone who would listen. "I'm going to fix them if I have to shove it down their throats!" It was a familiar scene in the weeks that followed as Nancy looked for every opportunity to bring her colleagues onside in defiance of the new regime.

To say that things did not go as Nancy had hoped would be an understatement. The warm, friendly greetings she used to get, if a little shallow at the time, soon vanished altogether. Lately it seemed every meeting and every presentation was Nancy against the world. And try as she did, they simply would not listen.

Still hopeful that one day she could bring the LaserNet team onside, Nancy saw a glimmer of hope when she got a meeting invite from Tom Smith, VP of sales operations. It had been almost exactly three months since the acquisition, and Tom was one of the more understanding operations executives on the LaserNet side. He had actually seemed to get some of what Nancy had been preaching.

Maybe we'll finally make some progress and get this ship moving in the right direction, Nancy thought optimistically as she entered the meeting room with renewed hope. Tom greeted her warmly and asked her to sit down. Another woman who Nancy had heard speak at the first company meeting was also there, which confused her a little. But before she could put all the pieces together, Nancy was given the bad news.

"Nancy, I'm sorry, but we're letting you go," Tom stated as quickly and stoically as he could. Clearly he wanted to leave no possible room for misinterpretation or interruption. "You've done great work, and everyone appreciates your passion and expertise. But honestly, it hasn't been as smooth a transition as we'd hoped, and we all feel it's time for you to move on. We want to wish you the best of luck in all your future endeavors."

Nancy's heart sank. She couldn't believe what she was hearing and skipped from shock straight to anger in about 10 seconds. "You idiots don't know what you're doing!" She fired back. "This is why you're getting killed in the market!" She was shouting now. "You wouldn't know great talent if it hit you in the face!" she pounded as she got up and stormed out of the room and into the parking lot. Her short career at LaserNet was over.

It wasn't until several years later that Nancy truly understood and accepted the mistakes she'd made. She took solace only in knowing she was neither the first, nor the last, to fall into this trap.

What We Can Learn From Nancy

Nancy learned one of the most important lessons for managing your career in business today. In comparison even to 20 years ago, change in corporations happens at a faster pace than most of us appreciate. As we'll continue to see in our stories, your best opportunities for advancement often present themselves in these times of uncertainty and transition. But at the same time, changing environments also bring the highest risk of career set-back if we don't approach them strategically.

Nancy's sad tale proves no amount of talent can protect you if you handle change poorly. The LaserNet team didn't care about the rightness or wrongness of her ideas. It was her attitude that got her fired. Why would they want to work with someone who was bound to be difficult or threatening to their way of life? Sure, the company may have benefited from a smart and talented process manager like Nancy, but companies are entities—aggregations; they don't make decisions. Human beings make the decisions that determine your fate.

Without a doubt, the winners and losers I've seen in my career have mostly had their fortunes determined in these moments of change. This is why it's so important to be at your best when they occur. We saw, in Nancy, a person with a predisposition to reject change, so when the moment presented itself, she chose to fight instead of embrace it.

This is a lesson that is a lot easier to write about than it is to put into practice. Emotions run so high in periods of transition it's very hard to maintain control. Often our personal wealth, our work, our friends, and our careers hang in the balance. So the temptation for Nancy, like for many of us, was to fight to preserve the old culture or brand or process. This temptation gets amplified by the herd dynamic as groups of the old guard band together to stand in opposition of the new normal. The fruitlessness of this reaction sounds obvious when we study it after the fact, but I still see it happen every time.

Nancy also showed us how career momentum can turn on a dime in the contemporary corporate environment. Your talent and expertise have very little ultimately to do with your upward mobility on this dynamic playing field. Nobody would call into question Nancy's intellect or her ability to execute, but she still wound up getting laid off. Termination is not a fate reserved for the untalented. One moment Nancy had been making great progress and the next moment she was out. The question for us is, How do we avoid falling into Nancy's trap?

Nancy's biggest mistake was reacting emotionally in the moment instead of formulating a plan designed to make her a long-term winner. She tried to fight against the tide and win every small battle she encountered. When you find yourself debating every issue or arguing with colleagues at meetings, you need to ask yourself honestly if this is a winning strategy in the long run. In Nancy's case, the answer was obviously no.

You never want to engage in a battle of any kind at work without a strong base. It was one thing for Nancy to ruffle a few feathers and challenge her colleagues when she had three years under her belt and was in good standing at EastStar. But after the LaserNet acquisition, she had none of that. Any points she'd scored at EastStar were wiped from the board. They didn't know her. They had no context for her processes or ideas. It is not surprising they rejected her plans and ultimately her value to the company. They were the acquiring company, so it stands to reason they would want to preserve their own culture and processes. Rather than fight, Nancy needed to find opportunities to embrace the change.

Nancy's final misstep was to opt for "what is right" over "what is right for my career." Arguing concepts and ideas and plans until you get terminated doesn't do you any good, whether you are right or not. Your priority at work is to get ahead, to improve your station in the corporation. If you do that, one day you can have influence and power and all the benefits that come with it. The mistake many of us, including Nancy, make is to play our hand prematurely. We over value the importance of being right before we've attained the power we need to safely influence our own rightness.

———

Let's take a look at the story of one of Nancy's colleagues who went through the very same acquisition but came out of it with a completely different result.

The Tale of Carl the Chameleon

As soon as the CEO said, "We've had our share of difficult decisions to make," Carl sensed they were in for a surprise. He had been through several liquidation events in the past, and he knew they never went as smoothly as people predicted.

In the moments immediately following the announcement, Carl couldn't help but flash back to his first real management job and how poorly he'd reacted when his company merged with another firm. *Probably set me back three years,* he shrugged off rather easily, having gone over it so many times in his head before. *But not this time.*

Redemption Plan

What most of his friends and colleagues didn't realize was that Carl, who was a senior account manager at EastStar, had spent most of the last five years trying to bounce back from a major career setback. He had been turfed after a legendary sequence of mistakes and misjudgments following the acquisition of his last firm. *I just couldn't accept the fact that these strangers were coming in and telling me how to do my job,* he remembered. *Changing up all our accounts, our systems, our travel policies.* But he knew now how wrong that attitude was. It had resembled denial more closely than career strategy.

Looking back, Carl often felt embarrassed that he allowed his emotions to dictate his tactics. What stung the most is how he watched a couple of his less-talented colleagues get raises and promotions during the same period. But Carl had taken his medicine and accepted the hard lessons from that moment. He vowed that when a similar situation next presented itself, he'd be ready. And he was.

Carl's preparation for this moment had started several months earlier. As soon as he had heard the company was planning to go public, Carl had started to piece together his strategy. No matter how it went down, he knew things would get crazy. People would change jobs and exit the company. Processes and roles and responsibilities would change very quickly. Most people wouldn't handle it well. So he planned his tactics:

1. *Be helpful.* Make the change easier on the acquiring company or new managers.

2. *Be friendly.* Find as many opportunities as possible to network with new people.

3. *Be positive.* Don't spend time or be seen spending time with disgruntled team members.

4. *Be patient.* Wait to gain a solid foothold before creating conflict or debating issues.

5. *Be visible.* Show up to work early and stay late for the first three months after the acquisition.

Even though he'd just scribbled these notes on the back of a cocktail napkin, Carl had his head on straight this time and felt confident his plan would work. The napkin sat in his drawer for the next 90 days. Now it was time.

On the evening before the presumed IPO announcement, Carl laid out the navy pinstripe suit he'd closed so many big deals in. As an account manager, he was no stranger to big moments. He slept confidently knowing he'd be ready to play his A-game no matter what happened the following morning.

Game Time

The meeting closed and immediately everyone on the EastStar side started mulling around in shock. They talked among themselves, speculating what it would all mean for their jobs and their stock options. Not Carl. He started executing his plan. It didn't take 30 seconds from the close of the presentation for Carl to make his first move. He parted from the herd, and immediately walked up to the stage and greeted their new owners, who had been left alone rather rudely while the EastStar staff collectively panicked.

"Hi. My name is Carl," he confidently broke the ice. *Put on your best "happy" face, he reminded himself.* "I've heard so many great things about LaserNet. I can't tell you how excited I am to be joining the team."

"Hey, Carl. Great to meet you. My name is Jeff Guthrie and I'm CEO of LaserNet. And this is the team." He led Carl toward the other LaserNet executives. "Great to be working with you, too."

Of course, Carl hadn't heard a peep about LaserNet for the better part of a decade and on the inside he was as concerned as everyone else. God only knew what merging with this dino-saur meant for the future of the company. But unlike his peers, Carl refused to let his emotions get in the way of his career playbook. Good company, bad company—it didn't matter. He had a plan and he was going see it through.

Things continued on in this way for several weeks. Carl proceeded to book meetings with every important LaserNet executive that would talk to him. He ate lunch with them. He went for after-work cocktails. He talked accounts and strategy, and showed every ounce of fake enthusiasm he could summon. And he was the only one. His peers grumbled and worried and were otherwise inhospitable to their new owners. Evidently they forgot who bought whom and refused to acknowledge the reality of the new power dynamics. But Carl didn't pay any attention to what everyone else was doing. In fact, he did his best to keep his distance from the worst of the herd so as not to mistakenly get lumped in with them. He chose not to react even when he caught a few of his colleagues making fun at his expense for "sucking up" to the LaserNet brass.

We'll see who wins in the long run, he reassured himself.

A Second Chance

Things continued to play out this way for the next two months. Carl tried his best to seem helpful and friendly to his new colleagues, while his peers longed audibly for the old days. And then, precisely 90 days after the fateful all-hands meeting, the inevitable reorganization e-mail shown on page 93 went out.

Carl was on cloud nine. He knew his teammates would say he'd been sucking up and playing politics. Carl didn't care. He was a director now and he'd finally gotten his career back on track.

Greetings LaserNet Family,

It's been an exciting three months as we've welcomed our new friends into the family. I know it hasn't been easy on everyone but I'm proud of the maturity you've shown and the hospitality you've demonstrated. As you know, we've spent this first 90 days making an assessment to determine how best to integrate the two companies, and we've got an exciting plan to share with you all. But before we do, we have some farewells to wish and some congratulations to extend.

We're sorry to be seeing Nancy Marquardt leave the company, and we want to thank her for all her contributions during the past three years....

Next, I'd like to take a moment to personally congratulate EastStar's very own Carl Williams who will be taking on the exciting new role of Global Account Director where he'll oversee all our joint strategic accounts. This is a very important role to me personally. As I've gotten to know Carl during the last few months I am certain he is the man for the job. Congrats, Carl!

Keep it up team! Looking forward to a bright future together.

Sincerely,

Jeff Guthrie, CEO, LaserNet

Your Personal Playbook: Embrace the Changes Everyone Else Hates

I've seen stories like this more times in my career than I can count. Nancy's fight against change is played out in corporations every day. It's our default response when uncertainty and transition define the playing field. It's rare to see managers get it right the first time. It took me two painful mistakes before I finally learned how to handle these situations the correct way. It probably set my career back five years. Whether it's an acquisition, an IPO, a management change, or a restructuring, the same principles apply.

Here are three quick tips that will make sure you embrace the changes everyone else hates and ultimately end up on top:

- Make a change plan. You need to actually write down what your plan is or your emotions will likely get the best of you. Jot down some tactics when a major transition occurs to force yourself to act strategically and not emotionally.

- Pick the winner with your mind, not your heart. Make an objective assessment of which side is likely to come out on top and join that team. If someone has just bought your company or has just taken over your department, choose that team. Don't fight against the winning side.

- Leave your ego at the door. If you execute the correct change playbook, people will make fun of you and tease you for being a suck-up. Ignore them. Your career is not about making friends; it's about advancement.

3. Learn to Promote Your Projects

In this section, we're going to hear the stories of Evan and Peter. Their tales deal with a trap I see people fall into all the time, in spite of the fact nearly every manager I know is aware of it. Evan's story comes from my own experience as a young product marketing manager. Peter's story comes from an old colleague who first taught me this valuable lesson. These stories address a scenario that applies to virtually every department and every company. I've used a couple of marketing examples, but they could just as easily take place in engineering or product management or sales. We're going to witness how the success of a project is influenced much more profoundly by how it is promoted internally than it is by the work itself. If we do our promotion effectively, we can insure ourselves against poor results.

The Tale of Evan the Invisible

Evan slowed down just enough to grab the *New York Times,* which was sticking a little more than an inch outside of the yellow box at the end of his driveway. It was 7:30 a.m. and he'd just completed a 7-mile run, as was his standard during the week. What few people knew is that Evan was a very talented runner and probably could have competed at the city or state level, even now in his early 30s. In truth, there were lots of things nobody knew about Evan. He was a humble guy and never wanted to make it "all about him," like so many of his friends were prone to do. It wasn't that Evan lacked self-confidence. He was good at almost everything—from sports to music to business. He just didn't like to brag about it.

Today was a big day for Evan, and he hoped it would come and go without any major surprises. As he changed out of his running clothes, showered, and donned his favorite cardigan, Evan daydreamed optimistically about how his mid-year performance review would go that morning.

Mixed Reviews

It had been six months since Evan had joined Future eCommerce in the role of product marketing manager, and he felt like he'd done a lot of good work already. There was no denying Evan had a lot of talent, and could create marketing content and campaigns like few others in the organization. It was quite evident to his marketing teammates and to his boss that Evan possessed a ton of potential, despite having only been with the company for a short period of time.

But not everyone at Future eCommerce had felt Evan's impact so profoundly. There had been a few occasions where managers from other departments had asked, only half in jest, about what Evan actually did for the company. Evan was well aware that this type of comment was not uncommon in reference to marketing personnel, yet it still gave him pause as he made the final preparations for his performance review.

As he walked into the office building well ahead of schedule, Evan carried measured confidence in with him. He had put a great deal of effort in over the course of the last six months and he was anxious to receive some validation. He looked forward to the 360-degree review that would take place later that morning.

"I just don't know what to make of this," mumbled Tara, the VP of marketing and Evan's boss. She was carrying a look of concern on her face. "Evan is so smart and his work is so good; I just don't understand how the feedback could be so... so...blah," she finished abruptly, feeling more than a little bewildered. It was puzzling to her how the marketing team could be so universally positive about Evan's performance and the rest of the company be so...indifferent.

Too confused to act, Tara decided to postpone Evan's review. She would do a little research into the situation before delivering the bad news to the man she had assumed was a rising star. After all, she wanted to be provide constructive feedback he could use to get better. But right now she was at a loss. From Tara's perspective, he was as smart as a whip and the model team player. She sent off the cancellation, put her proverbial detective hat on, and got down to work.

Promo Preparation

Evan didn't know what to make of the postponement but didn't really give it much thought, either. *I can't believe I wore my favorite cardigan for this,* he mocked himself in the restroom mirror, frankly, feeling a little relief. He understood how busy his boss could get, and it wasn't uncommon for her to postpone or cancel a meeting, even at the last minute. They were all busy. So he got back to work on his latest marketing campaign, a project he felt certain would generate a ton of sales leads for the next quarter.

Evan had been working on this promotional campaign for a month. He'd done all the research, all the design, all the media planning—everything. He'd spent nights and weekends planning and analyzing the campaign. He was proud of his work. Evan only had a few more days of prep ahead of him before the scheduled internal launch to the sales force at the end of the week. Whereas he may have been a little nervous for his performance review, this one he was supremely confident in.

Evan spent the final few days going over every last detail of the campaign in his mind. He'd analyzed past campaigns to see what had worked and what hadn't. He'd run the numbers on the expected revenue impact of the promotion. He'd researched best practices for similar promotions. He'd considered everything. Evan was so focused on his campaign he'd even canceled his regular weekly meeting with the sales managers. It had to be perfect.

On presentation day, Evan felt comfortable that he'd crossed every "t" and dotted every "i." His slides were polished. His program was fully baked. He was ready—or so he thought.

The Work Speaks for Itself?

Evan's voice seemed to crack over the conference line as he tried to recover from what seemed like an extraordinarily long pause to anyone on the other end of the call. Things were not going well. It had all started off as planned. He took the entire sales organization through his campaign. The plan, the execution—all of it well-thought-out and meticulously assembled by him personally. But he'd barely gotten through the first two slides of his presentation when the tough questions started piling on.

"What about the deals I have in the pipeline already? Won't they be negatively affected by this promo?" asked one of the large account sales executives.

"Woh! My distributors aren't going to go for this. They just did an identical promotion with another vendor," barked a senior merchandising manager.

"This isn't what customers really care about. It's like you've never been out in the field!" shouted one of the younger sales representatives somewhat inappropriately.

It kept on going for 30 minutes until finally Evan was given a partial reprieve from Tara who had been listening in.

"Okay, guys," Tara said with authority. "Let's all calm down. Why don't you give Evan and the team another week, and we'll come back with a second pass at this."

And so the meeting ended with Evan staring blankly into space not sure whether to run home and hide, or to start crying right there and then in the conference room.

How could this have gone so terribly wrong? It just doesn't make sense, Evan moaned to himself as he took off what was no longer his favorite cardigan. It all seemed so unfair and so confusing. Clearly they just didn't get it or they had it in for him personally. *Salespeople,* he muttered as he donned his running gear hoping to plan his next move out on the road.

What We Can Learn From Evan

Evan's story illustrates one of the most common mistakes we see made by highly talented managers and young executives. So often, we wrongfully assume the work speaks for itself. Even when we know in our hearts it's not enough just to do high-quality work, we feel like it should be. But in my experience, the success of any project or initiative is 40 percent about the quality of the work and 60 percent about the way in which it's promoted inside the company.

I've learned this lesson no less than 10 times in my career. There are rare cases even now where I get busy or distracted, and I am forced to learn it again. Any work you are doing that has impact on other people within the company, or where other people can influence all or part of its success, must be fully promoted. This is not, in and of itself, news to you. We've all heard this best practice before. It's very easy to nod your head as though it's an obvious business truism. But in practice, I just don't see managers abide by it. I'm writing a book on the subject and admittedly I still make this mistake from time to time. And if you take an honest assessment of your own habits, you'll likely find opportunities where you can do a more effective job promoting your work, too.

Failure to promote your work is not because you do not understand its importance. We all know we should do it. It's much more about having poorly ordered priorities and the wrong scorecard for project success. The temptation for smart, talented managers is always to focus on the work itself as the number-one priority. And we carry around a misguided confidence that if we try hard enough and do quality work, that will be enough. But quality of work is not enough on its own.

When things get busy and deadlines draw near, we are forced to focus on our top priorities only. Because quality of work is so often placed at the top, and internal promotion is so often placed at the bottom, we fall into the same trap time and again. We fool ourselves into some false assumptions that a) All the people who care about the project can tell the difference between good and bad work, and b) All the people who care about the project have the same definition of good and bad as we do. I see evidence every day that these statements are not an accurate reflection of how things actually work in a corporation.

If we look at Evan's story, the large account sales executive only cared about his current quarter's deals. He probably had a lot of commission riding on them to close without disruption. So for him, any hint of derailing his opportunities was going to cause a negative reaction. But Evan didn't take the time to calm his fears before the launch. For the senior merchandising manager, it was about his personal relationships with partners who support marketing campaigns from many vendors and might react poorly to duplicating one. But Evan had no clue this could be an issue. Finally, for the young sales representative it was about feeling listened to. But Evan hadn't taken the necessary steps to protect against this kind of emotional reaction.

We see these examples all the time. What makes it so frustrating for talented managers like Evan is they rarely have anything to do with the quality of the work itself. Evan was very sharp, and his team and boss knew it. But that's not what got him into trouble, and ultimately not what caused his campaign to fail before it ever left the door. What makes it even more frustrating is how easy it is to take the necessary steps to properly promote your work and ensure you never run into a scenario like Evan did. Perhaps more than any of the other lessons in this book, promoting your work is the easiest and fastest way to raise your game.

When we talk about project promotion, we need to focus on three types in particular: concept promotion, alignment promotion, and results promotion. They are equally important.

Concept promotion is about getting influencers excited about your work before you begin a project. When I say "influencers," I mean the three to five people inside or outside the company who have the most to win and lose from the success of your work. It should go without saying they need to actually have influence within the company to be on this list. You don't want to waste your time promoting work to lower level staff whose opinions aren't likely to sway the sentiment of the organization.

The key to effective concept promotion is to get a clear understanding of what your influencers care about, irrespective of your own project objectives. Once you understand this, you must articulate how a successful project will help them achieve their goals. It sounds simple enough, but it's not well executed in practice. What I see managers do over and over again is promote concepts from an inward looking perspective—promoting how *they* will win and why *they* think it's a good idea. Focus your concept promotion on expressing a vision of success in terms that reflect the perspectives of your influencers—not yourself.

Alignment promotion is about making people feel like they're on the inside. It's designed to avoid negative initial reactions, which can often be irrational—irrational, but still devastating, as we saw in Evan's case with the young sales rep. Emotional first responses can inject uncertainty into the project and derail otherwise positive momentum. Even a small amount of public negativity can open the flood gates to more negative sentiment as the herd dynamic takes hold. Alignment promotion protects against this.

Effective alignment promotion starts by expanding your list of three to five influencers to now include a second set of people I refer to as "potential disruptors." If you look around your own company, it's easy to spot these people. They're the ones asking all the questions in every company meeting and the ones who, on occasion, talk before thinking. Their default first reaction to anything is critical. You want to set aside time to walk these colleagues through everything you're going to present a few days before delivering it publicly. This way, they have time to process and ask all the questions they'd otherwise ask in public. You'll often hear managers talk about having a lot of questions after a presentation as though it were some indicator of success. I don't want any questions; I want to hear crickets when I'm done. If I've done my homework, I've answered all the potential questions several days earlier and I've properly aligned all the potential disruptors before I launch.

The last type of internal promotion is **results promotion**. Results promotion can act as an insurance policy against poor performance when done correctly. However, it is too often done selectively, which can be dangerous for you in the long term. Too many managers promote the positive results but not the negative results. This is a flawed strategy. It makes a few false assumptions, including: a) People don't notice when you only report good results, b) People actually care about the results themselves, and c) People will hold you accountable for poor results if you reveal them. If you have done your promotion correctly, none of these assumptions is true.

You need to report all types of results if you're going to be perceived to be objective. Objectivity is a powerful image to carry in your professional career, and it is scarce. You will find people don't really care about your results for the most part anyway. Normally they are too focused on their own priorities to care very much. In my experience, if you're objective, and you've properly promoted and aligned key influencers to your work before it launches, you won't be held accountable for poor results, because everyone will feel invested in the project personally. To assign blame on you would mean they would also take some accountability for the failure themselves. Nobody wants to do that.

———

In our next story about Peter the Promoter, we'll see an example of how proper promotion can actually make up for low-quality work when executed correctly. We'll see how internal alignment and promotion can make your colleagues and influencers *want* you to be successful and how it can protect you even when results are poor.

The Tale of Peter the Promoter

Peter was exhausted. He might have had three hours sleep the night before, which seemed to be the norm lately. But he was a passionate guy, and when he set his mind to something, Peter went all the way. The something in this case was his costume for the annual zombie march in town. Peter loved zombies. His friends loved zombies. And if he was honest with himself, he secretly longed for a post–zombie apocalypse world. He was ready for it, too. The only problem he faced was that between now and the zombie pandemic, Peter also had to work for a living. Every day it was becoming more of a struggle to stay motivated. So on this sunny Monday morning, as Peter slipped out of his one-piece zombie PJs and into his completely impractical business suit, his focus shifted momentarily to the program he was meant to launch later that week.

Dead Man Working

Aaron looked pensively at his computer screen. He had some serious doubts about his new hire, and it was distracting him. It had only been 90 days, but he'd seen none of the promise he saw glimmers of during Peter's interview process. He'd come so highly recommended as a professional services manager, which made it all the more frustrating that the guy seemingly didn't care about services in the slightest. Peter had managed to eke out a decent first project, but Aaron suspected it was because people were going easy on the new guy. He was pretty certain his next project would be a disaster. As he looked over Peter's work one last time, Aaron cringed at the thought of what was likely to come Friday afternoon.

What Aaron didn't know about his new employee was that what Peter lacked in professional services prowess and passion, he made up for in zombie fighting skills. They would come in handy when the inevitable came to pass. And a big part of fighting zombies, as everyone knows, is preparing for the unexpected. This is where Peter really excelled. Truth be told, Peter had spent less than a day working on the new service offering he was meant to pitch to the sales force later that week. But he'd spent a full hour talking it over with Jenna and Michael from the sales team over lunch and felt pretty confident they were all on the same page.

In actual fact, what got Peter turned onto this program in the first place was a conversation he'd had several weeks back with one of the other sales managers. As it happens, Jeff, who ran the Eastern region, was a zombie enthusiast himself, albeit more a *Walking Dead* follower than a *Night of the Living Dead* connoisseur. *Newbies,* Peter recalled as he thought back on their encounter. On that evening, in between makeup and marching sessions, Peter had floated the concept for his program mostly to get Jeff to stop yammering on about work. It seemed Jeff was preoccupied with the problems his internal professional services reps were experiencing. All his talk was cutting into valuable zombie time, so Peter had thrown out a few rough ideas. It was early days to say the least, but Jeff certainly seemed to be aligned with the broad strokes.

Today's lunch with Jenna and Michael had been enlightening as well, although it was a little tense for a moment or two.

Peter wanted to make sure he was on the right track, and he knew Jenna in particular could be a bit critical and extremely vocal in her disenchantment when it occurred. He heard several of the same issues Jeff had raised at the zombie event but with a measurably different perspective.

"Our partners are dying out there," said Jenna, with a little too much drama in her words.

"There isn't enough services revenue to sustain the channel," Michael added a little more objectively. "We need a way to drive more services business without compromising our partners."

Kill me. And do it with proper zombie technique. Make sure you sever my head. It took less than five minutes with Jenna and Michael for Peter to realize he had been headed in a direction that would have had the complete opposite impact to what they wanted. He had been focused on the internal services team when all along it was the services partners he needed to target. Peter had to restrain himself from bolting out of the restaurant right there and then. But he quickly regained composure and made a decision to change his program on the spot.

"Absolutely agree," Peter said with faux conviction as he fought the urge to run out of the room. "And that's why my new services offering can only be sold by our business partners and not by us directly." He was making things up as he went along. "Now is not the time to be competing with our own partners, and I sincerely hope this small step will send our company in a new direction," he brought it home, now really starting to feel it. As he laid out the rest of his real-time plan Peter thanked his lucky stars he'd had this conversation in advance of the launch presentation.

The Reckoning

Peter finished delivering three of the worst presentation slides Aaron had ever seen. It wasn't that the ideas were terrible—they weren't great—but they were so obviously rushed and half baked. As Peter paused and handed it over to the audience for comments, Aaron felt a wave of uneasiness pass over him. *This isn't going to be pretty*, he told himself like a man cornered by a group of zombies. He braced for impact.

"I just want to say how refreshing that was," bellowed the sales vice president, who couldn't have possibly seen the same presentation Aaron had witnessed. "Finally someone in services is thinking about growing our partner business. I love it."

"Here, here!" Jenna chimed from the phone. "This is exactly what we need in the field."

"This is great work, Peter," boomed a voice that Aaron was pretty sure belonged to the company's COO, the ultimate confirmation of success. "We're lucky to have you on board."

Peter fielded a few more straightforward questions and closed up the call feeling good about himself and frankly relieved that he could go home early to finish off his zombie walk costume. A perplexed but pleased Aaron shook his head and decided to give Peter the benefit of the doubt going forward.

Your Personal Playbook: Learn to Promote Your Projects

The stories of Evan and Peter remind us how important it is to promote our projects with key influencers. Promotion is so vital it can often alter the perception of high- and low-quality work. For all intents and purposes, Evan put a ton of time and thought into his campaign, yet it died on the vine. He prioritized research and analysis over promotion and alignment. Peter, on the other hand, spent next to no time on the work but made sure he presented something his audience wanted to hear. And with so many influencers on board, even a failed project wasn't going to hurt Peter in the end. Here are a few tips you can use to make sure you never forget that promotion is your number-one project priority:

- Know your influencers. Make sure you know the three to five people who have the most influence on your project's success and failure. Look for outspoken people and individuals who tend to be critical.

- Promote three times. Good promotion starts with getting people onside with the basic concept. Then it's about giving a sneak peek to bring critical people onto your team. Last, it's about objectively promoting the results for everyone to share in its success or failure.

- Promotion is the priority. When you get busy, you'll be tempted to forego promotion. It's much safer to sacrifice the work instead. Invest what little time you have in preparing your audience and taking the risk out of the presentation.

4. Avoid the Farce of Results Orientation

In this section, we're going to hear the stories of Polly and Jack. Without question, this is the lesson that gets the most resistance from managers I counsel. To follow it requires a level of personal discipline most of us struggle to find. These two tales come from the early part of my career when I certainly did not possess that self-discipline. It wasn't until many years later that I grasped the important distinctions between the mindsets of Polly and Jack, and how one small change in priorities can literally mean the difference between success and failure for a manager. Let's go through their stories, and we can examine what is to be learned from their career strategies and ultimately their fates.

The Tale of Polly the Performer

It was a beautiful Monday morning in Silicon Valley. The sound of early-morning lawn mowers told you everything you needed to know about the weather. As soon as she woke up, Polly knew this was her day. She could barely get to sleep last night after she got the e-mail from Nelson, her boss and mentor. A somewhat cryptic subject line— "Discuss New Opportunities"—could only mean one thing, couldn't it? After two years of long hours and countless sacrifices to her sorry excuse for a social life, Polly was going to get her promotion. And she deserved it, too.

Just Desserts

Polly worked for a company called 9vine.com, one of the hot social media ventures causing buzz in the Valley. The company was growing rapidly, and the pressures of continuous expansion reverberated in every department. Though Polly was certainly not alone in feeling the pressure, she felt it in spades every day. As content marketing manager, Polly's job was extremely demanding and required every ounce of energy she could summon on a day-to-day basis.

Whereas Polly could envision how her hard work and high stress would pay off in the end, others around her could not. For months now, Polly's friends and family had been urging her to bail on Nelson and find a new job. She just seemed so tired all the time. But that was not Polly. She had stuck by Nelson through thick and thin.

Admittedly, Nelson could be a bit of a tyrant, and to say he was results oriented would be the understatement of the year. He was myopically focused on the numbers, and he demanded the same from his staff. If it didn't involve something measurable that he could report for the current quarter, Nelson didn't want to hear about it. Polly's entire existence was about making the numbers. This sometimes seemed a bit confusing to her, because they were in the marketing department and frequently wanted to take a longer-term view of things.

There was no point in lying to herself. There were days when it didn't seem worth it to Polly. Nelson could be a bear and she spent 95 percent of her time trying to figure out how to hit his performance metrics. In her few quiet moments, Polly sometimes worried she wasn't learning to be a better marketer in the process. Yes, she had learned how to drive more visits to the Website and how to raise their search ranking on Google, but sometimes she had to suppress the little voice in her head that told her there might be a bigger picture she was missing.

None of that matters now, Polly smiled. Today she'd be ready for anything—every number, every result. Anything they wanted to know, she would be prepared. Polly had been longing for this day for what felt like an eternity. She started to relax for the first time in two years.

Change, of Course

Polly quickly decided she ought to dress the part. A special day demanded a special outfit. As she donned her favorite power suit, Polly couldn't help but let her mind wander to how she would spend the salary increase, and what she might do with all that new office space. What almost nobody else knew is that Polly had been dreaming of buying her own home but she just couldn't afford it—*Until now*, she sighed, more from relief than anything else. It was going to be a great day; Polly was sure of that.

The 9vine.com office seemed livelier than normal. As Polly walked into the building and made her way to the meeting room, she couldn't help but notice all the young people milling around, seemingly having a great time for 9:30 a.m. Frankly she'd spent so much time with her head down on tasks she didn't get a chance to socialize with her colleagues as much as she might have liked. For all the talk in the press about what a great culture the company had, Polly rarely got to experience it.

Polly entered the meeting room a little early, intending to wait for Nelson, who did not tolerate tardiness. She was not alone. But just as Polly was about to introduce herself to the stranger sitting in front of her, a commotion erupted outside the room.

Nelson still had a look of shock on his face as he marched past the meeting room where Polly and an unfamiliar woman were sitting. He could see a look of bewilderment on Polly's face as he walked sheepishly by with a box of his belongings in hand.

"Not enough e-commerce experience," he muttered to himself as he left the building in a haze, wondering how this could have happened.

Evidently someone had decided the company needed to adjust their sales channels to focus on e-commerce, but Nelson was a content guy. All his hard work seemed to be for nothing now. He'd been driving traffic to the site like a champ for the past two years, and all of a sudden it seemed nobody cared.

In fairness to Nelson's superiors, they had been very compassionate. They acknowledged his value and his expertise, but had decided to go in another direction. Effective immediately, he was being let go, and they were going to replace him. Evidently, his successor's name was Diane, and she had been in e-commerce for more than two decades. "I'm pretty sure two decades ago it was just called 'commerce'," he had said in the meeting before calming himself down. But from what they said, Diane would be able to really hit the ground running.

As Nelson stumbled into the parking lot, he couldn't help but look back with an ounce of regret on the countless evenings and weekends he'd spent with Polly meticulously driving those traffic numbers. *Poor Polly*, he thought. *I hope she lands on her feet*.

From the moment she sat down, Polly knew something was terribly wrong. Questions raced through her mind: *Where is Nelson? Who is this strange woman beside me? Why can't I stop sweating through this power suit?*

It didn't take long to get the answers to her first two questions. They became painfully clear as a pale-looking Nelson walked past, box in hand, in what seemed to be a near-catatonic state.

"Am I getting fired?" Polly blurted across the conference room table without introducing herself or taking a minute to regain composure.

In the 15 minutes that followed, she commenced a journey that would end by learning a valuable but painful lesson that she would never forget.

It was all a blur. Polly later recollected: "The company has made some changes." "We're shaking things up a bit." "We know you've done some great work here, but…." "It's all about e-commerce now." "We're hoping you'll be able to hit the ground running." Only still images and sound bites had made it through to her.

One thing was perfectly clear: Nelson had been replaced and Polly would be assuming a new role focused on e-commerce. She would be reporting to Diane. Polly felt simultaneously relieved and trepidatious. *E-commerce*, she thought. *I don't know the first thing about e-commerce. I've just spent the last two years of my life driving Web traffic*.

Her first meeting with Diane was awkward to say the least. "We're over a hundred thousand visits a month!" Polly had yelped at one point in the meeting in response to an unrelated question. She had an overwhelming urge to prove her worth right out of the gate. What she heard in response nearly made her sick to her stomach, and seemed to foreshadow the future relationship she'd have with her new boss.

"That's great," Diane had said in a somewhat patronizing tone, "But how is that translating to sales?"

Just Like That

In the days that followed, Polly experienced a wide range of emotions, which for the most part landed near the panic end of the spectrum. She hadn't hit it off with Diane at all, and it was beginning to become apparent that Polly had very little experience or acumen for e-commerce. It didn't help matters much that Diane had almost no time or patience to help her through the concepts. Diane expected someone of Polly's experience level to have e-commerce expertise and seemed to be growing frustrated by her lack of progress.

Making matters worse, Polly was not handling the change well emotionally. In retrospect, she lamented this misstep in particular. She found herself debating with Diane all the time, and sometimes she caught herself pushing back on some pretty insignificant issues. It was as though she was in competition with her own boss to prove her value. But every time she tried, it seemed to backfire. She couldn't help herself. When she replayed it all later Polly realized how fruitless it had been to challenge her new boss in this way, but she had worked so hard for the previous two years with Nelson and she had been so close to that big promotion. Surely that should have counted for something. But it didn't.

Whenever the opportunity presented itself, Polly made a point of referencing the great things she'd done in the past, and how she'd delivered results and met targets like clockwork. She tried to show off all the tips and tricks and best practices she and Nelson had built, but for some reason, Diane never seemed to care that much. Yes, she nodded and seemed to acknowledge the successes on occasion, but it clearly didn't seem relevant to Diane's agenda.

Two months went by without improvement in Polly's relationship with Diane. Her e-commerce acumen was not improving much either. It was just too much to expect her to learn everything there was to know about e-commerce in a couple of months. There had been more than a few regrettable arguments with Diane stemming from her unrealistic expectations.

Exactly 90 days after Nelson's termination, Polly got the inevitable call. Diane invited Polly into her office to deliver the bad news.

"Polly, I'm sorry to tell you the company has decided to let you go." Diane looked sincerely empathetic. "As you know, it's all about e-commerce now and we really need someone who can hit the ground running. We appreciate your hard work on the site, but it's time for a change."

The exit meeting lasted all of two minutes. Polly had little to say. She had feared this day would come. Although Polly was not surprised in the least at this point, and frankly resigned to this inevitability, she couldn't help but bemoan the vicious turn of fate that had befallen her—from two years of dogged work delivering results for Nelson, to being certain of a promotion, to sitting in the meeting room wearing that ridiculous power suit, to being fired. All in the blink of an eye.

It all seemed so unfair.

What We Can Learn From Polly

For many of you, Polly's story should hit close to home. On the surface, it may seem like Polly just had a run of bad luck. But that is not what caused her demise. Polly lost because she became a one-trick pony. Her fate demonstrates the risk of focusing too much on one specialized skill and of fixating on delivering short-term results. Organizational change is inevitable. It's also on the rise as companies move faster with every passing year. You need to be prepared for it.

Polly can teach us a valuable lesson if we choose to accept it. I underscore that last point, because her lesson is perhaps the most difficult for talented managers and young executives to embrace.

Results orientation is one of the most universally accepted business mantras, but it serves everyone's interest other than your own. As we saw with Polly, when we fixate on delivering results, we are choosing to ignore working on what will actually get us ahead in the long run. Polly made a choice, although it may not have seemed like one at the time, to forego broadening her expertise in exchange for delivering short-term results for Nelson. And by doing this, she became too heavily leveraged both to Nelson's personal success (to carry her along with him) and also to generating Website traffic as her only real professional skill.

Without knowing it, Polly became what I call a "Super Specialist," which is the business equivalent to a one-trick pony. It's the opposite of the often-successful Jack of All Trades we examined earlier. Playing the Super Specialist game plan is a heavily leveraged career strategy. It carries considerable risk, which outweighs the potential upside of winning with the strategy. The upside of specializing to this degree is that if your skill remains valuable you'll always have a role to play. On the other hand, there are two serious downside risks that make this a bad strategy to adopt.

First, by specializing on one set of results or one set of skills you are making a bet that they will always be relevant to the company or the industry. What Polly found out the hard way is that when the company makes big, sudden, strategic changes, which they so often do, your specialty, and you by extension, can quickly become irrelevant. I have seen this play out in my own areas of expertise just in the last few years. My profession of marketing has undergone massive change and its leaving some people behind. Social media and mobile communications have fundamentally changed the way consumers purchase goods and services. As a result, there is an entire generation of marketers who now stare extinction in the face. If you're not actively broadening your skills as part of your daily routine, you're making a critical mistake.

The second downside risk to this level of specialization is that you narrow the position you hold within the perceptions of your superiors. A narrow position is a bad one because nobody can picture you anywhere other than in your current role. And it doesn't matter much how good you happen to be at it. Every employee owns a position in the minds of his or her superiors. In Polly's case, she was the Web traffic guru, and when the company directive changed to e-commerce it was impossible to alter that perception. Granted, Polly didn't help matters the way she behaved in her new role, but changing perception is a slow-moving process and difficult to accomplish.

These are two good examples of why you need to allocate more time to broadening your skill set and spend less time fixated on delivering results. The average person now works for almost a dozen different companies in his or her lifetime.[1] Your career success and failure will play out across them all. You just can't over-commit your time and energy to immediate term priorities. Polly learned this the hard way.

I've personally experienced the frustration of working tirelessly for years to deliver results for my manager only to have him or her replaced by someone new. That's when you learn your results don't transition from one boss or company to another. Ultimately, in every new career situation, you will be viewed from a different lens, their lens. Focusing on expanding our skills and learning to navigate the human element of a corporation are far more valuable investments in your career than short term results delivery. They travel well.

We see results orientation manifest in all its favorite forms: "Just net it out for me," "How can I tie this back to revenue?", "It's all about the numbers," and "We need to build a performance culture."

We've all said these things, and we hear and follow them as business gospel. No manager in her right mind would ever dream about questioning the logic behind these directives because to do so in the wrong company would seem like committing career suicide. But like all innovation, making change to your career strategy starts with questioning the norm.

Is it really all about the numbers? Why am I always "netting" things out? Why am I tying everything I do back to revenue?

Results have a short shelf life. Skills have value over many years and roles. Look at your resume; does anyone really care that you increased sales pipeline by 34 percent seven years ago at a company they didn't even work for? And even if that is somewhat impressive, does it matter at all that it's 34 percent and not 31 percent? I would argue it doesn't. On the other hand, learning a new selling approach or developing your skills in contract negotiation will apply to many future roles you may hold.

So when making choices on what to invest your time in at work, you need to consider which investments will deliver the best return for your career when viewed with a multi-company, multi-manager lens.

———

What we'll see in our next story about Jack the Generalist is an example of how a career game plan that is less heavily leveraged on results orientation can work in your favor.

The Tale of Jack the Generalist

It was freezing. Jack always struggled to justify living on the East Coast when he returned from a trip somewhere warm. His cramped, cold apartment just didn't seem as glamorous as "Manhattan studio loft" sounded. But cold or not, as he unpacked his suitcase, Jack still felt a glow from the week he'd just spent in Las Vegas.

Jack had just spent the week at SoTech, the world's foremost social media marketing conference. He had been looking forward to it for months—not so much for the Vegas factor like his friends and family joked, but because he truly enjoyed having some dedicated time to learn new things. Jack had lobbied hard for the budget and time to attend, and it had been totally worth it. Irene, his boss, had been reluctant, to put it mildly. She just didn't see the value in that kind of training and probably suspected Jack was spending more time at the craps table than the conference itself. *But what an experience it was*, he recalled to himself as he deleted some of the less-appropriate photos from his camera.

What happens in Vegas.... He smiled to himself.

A Pair of Jacks

Jack was addicted to learning. In fairness, it was often at the expense of his work on a day-to-day basis. On paper, his job was Senior Project Manager, Web Properties, which was a very long way of saying he was just like everyone else at Tiger Brand Partners. But for the past two years, he had been leading a double life. He did just enough to meet his performance objectives while steadily acquiring new skills and knowledge and using the company to pay for most of it. In fact, he had spent an inordinate amount of time during the last three quarters researching and learning new digital marketing techniques. For all intents and purposes, Jack had basically gotten his MBA at work—albeit from Google University. Surely Irene would have to stand up and take notice soon.

Jack recalled so many great experiences from the event—the night of dueling pianos and Ukrainian acrobats notwithstanding. One encounter in particular stuck with him. Jack had fortuitously run into Bill Matthews, their global vice president of marketing. He was attending the event and had been happy to spend some time with Jack while they were there. Bill was more of a legend than a real person to Jack and his peers. He'd actually never even met the man until this past week. He was happy to have had the chance to spend a little time with their iconic leader, even if it was only for a short while.

As energized as Jack was from his experience, he had received a rather cryptic meeting request earlier that evening. It held the subject line "New Opportunities," which sounded like those generic meeting requests that always seemed to precede a layoff or transfer. But there was no sense in worrying about it now. Jack vowed not to let anything get in the way of his master plan.

Winner, Winner, Chicken Dinner

Jack's relationship with his boss was livable for the most part, although she occasionally criticized him for getting sidetracked. Irene wanted him more focused on Website performance and ensuring they ranked highly in searches. This seemed to be her *raison d'être*. Jack had to give her credit, though: Irene hit her performance numbers every quarter. As a team, they had nailed the Web traffic objective for five quarters in a row. If there was one thing Irene was truly great at it, was search engine optimization.

In spite of his boss's obsession with Web metrics, Jack could never shake the feeling that there had to be more. His daily routine just didn't offer him the chance to learn enough to get him where he wanted to go. In his master plan, Jack was going to be a VP of marketing in the next five years, but there was no way anyone would consider him for that job if all he knew was how to generate Website traffic. So he studied and researched and went to conferences to learn about all the aspects of marketing. He wanted to be a well-rounded manager.

Unfortunately for Jack, sometimes his passion for learning came at the expense of his performance metrics. He'd missed a couple monthly targets recently, and there was tension once in a while between him and Irene. It was nothing serious, but it was clear she felt he was toeing the line with his extracurricular activities. He made a deal with himself that if he didn't get fired the next day, he'd make sure to spend some quality time with Irene and on the Web traffic in the next couple weeks before taking on his next personal learning initiative.

The next morning, Jack showed up to his meeting five full minutes late. He was known for his tardiness, and it often did not sit well with Irene. But it didn't matter this time, as he found himself completely alone in the conference room.

Where the heck is Irene? he wondered, growing impatient and wishing for a moment he hadn't deleted those pictures off his phone. But before he could daydream any longer, the answer to his question marched past him.

As she stormed past the meeting room, Irene looked pissed. She had the look of someone who had just said and done things she regretted. *How could they?* She tossed a dirty look through the window at Jack, who sat unawares in a meeting room looking confused and concerned. As her anger and disbelief slowly turned into sadness, Irene wondered how this could have happened to her.

Evidently, the company needed to shake things up. The Wall Street analysts said they weren't embracing social media enough and were rapidly becoming a dinosaur in the industry. *A dinosaur?* Irene was laughing to herself with more than a little venom. *We're a software company, for goodness sake.*

But nevertheless, Tiger Brand Partners wanted to go in a different direction. The management team had decided that in spite of her great efforts, they needed someone leading the charge with more experience in social media marketing. As painful as that was to hear for Irene, what really hurt was what happened next.

Jack had a front-row seat for Irene's epic departure. He watched in amazement and concern for his boss as she stormed past the meeting room he was seated in—box in hand, wearing a dazzling power suit, and yelling all manner of obscenities at everyone and anyone.

Holy doodle, he thought to himself. Jack realized immediately they must be doing layoffs. And he must be next! If someone like Irene who made her numbers every quarter was gone, he certainly must be gone, too.

As he pictured his master career plan going up in smoke, Bill, the vice president of marketing, who he'd run into earlier in the week, walked in and sat down beside him.

"I'm sorry you had to see that, Jack," Bill said. "Irene is a good person and a hard worker, and we're sorry to see her go. But we've got to shake things up and get into the 21st century."

"Am I fired?" Jack blurted before he could think of something intelligent to say.

"Fired? Oh, no, Jack; I apologize," Bill said as though he may have missed a memo somewhere in the process. "I didn't mean to scare you. We'd like you to run the department moving forward. We know you've got the social media expertise we need, and you've got the experience here to really hit the ground running. Can we count on you?"

And just like that, Jack's life had taken an amazing turn. From all those months trying to justify why he was late with the metrics and a bit short on his numbers, and all the time he spent trying to expand his skills, he was finally there.

Though Jack couldn't help but feel sadness for Irene, he smiled quietly to himself. His master plan was going to be a reality.

Your Personal Playbook: Avoid the Farce of Results Orientation

We learned a lot from the stories of Polly and Jack. Many of you will have had similar experiences in your own career. This lesson may seem counterintuitive and very different from what your colleagues are doing, but that is the point. You need to avoid being overly leveraged on results orientation. You need to purposefully invest time in expanding your skill set while you're at work. This is your best protection from company, departmental, and management changes. An investment in skills will pay dividends for much longer than an investment in results. In five years, nobody will care about your results this quarter, but they will care about the skills and tools you possess. Here are three key tactics you can add to your career strategy that will ensure you properly invest your time and energy at work:

- Reallocate your time. Favor skills expansion over results delivery. Spend 20 to 30 percent of every day learning new skills with the intention of broadening your expertise versus specializing in any one area.

- Expand your perceived position. Make a point of telling people what you're learning and the progress you're making. They need to be able to imagine you in other roles with wider responsibilities.

- Play the long game. Your career plays out over many companies and bosses. Never tie your future to one person or one skill set. In today's rapidly changing corporations, you need to favor skill flexibility over skill depth.

5. Don't Be a Part of the Herd

In this section, we're going to hear the stories of Gary and Larry. I've seen stories just like theirs play out many times in my career. Gary's story comes from one of my first management experiences and Larry's tale took place in the middle part of my career, in a period where I was truly tested. They are great examples of how emotional control can be all that separates you from getting ahead in your career or getting left behind—so powerful, in fact, that Incompetent Executives use this attribute to overcome their often glaring lack of talent. As managers, we tend to pay lip service to these soft skills, but as we'll see, they can make all the difference. These tales illustrate a very common mistake lower-level staff and managers make when they allow their emotions to dictate their career strategies. Let's take a look at how two individuals with opposing mindsets ultimately earned opposing fates.

The Tale of Gary the Gossiper

Gary couldn't remember a happier time in his career. He'd finally found a place that felt like home. For the first time,

Gary actually looked forward to going to work in the morning. He had joined G-Tech Inc. almost two years ago, and it had been a great ride already. His role as digital marketing manager gave him the opportunity to work with a team full of people he liked. And Gary was well aware that he was considered by some to be a rising star in the organization for the impact he'd had on their digital strategy.

Business BFFs

In many ways, Gary's work life on a day-to-day basis felt a little more like his college years than an actual job. He and his teammates spent so much time laughing and joking, it almost seemed wrong to call what they did "work," which is not to say they weren't performing. In fact, the entire team was talented, and their performance reflected it. At this point, Gary had become so used to his congenial work environment, he honestly now had trouble relating to friends and family who seemed so unhappy all the time. Gary felt truly blessed to have such a great job. Better still, he felt he was almost certainly next in line for the highly coveted director position that was budgeted for the beginning of next year.

To be fair, it wasn't all roses at work for Gary. His boss, Jiro, for example, was extremely difficult to work with. Jiro seemed to lack any marketing expertise or acumen by any measure Gary and his teammates could muster. At times, it even seemed like Jiro might be losing it in the way he seemed to jump from one priority to the next. He ran around the office barking orders like he was an NFL quarterback calling an audible at the line of scrimmage. Jiro was so crass and so difficult to work with, Gary and his teammates had recently taken to calling him "Jiro the zero"—behind his back, of course. But on the upside, Gary told himself—and his peers reassured him— *When they let Jiro go I'll be first in line for his job.*

As the fiscal year wound to a close, Gary and his friends— colleagues I mean—were growing increasingly skeptical of Jiro's competency as a manager. At the same time, they were growing increasingly bold in their griping and joking at his expense. A couple times, even Gary felt uncomfortable with some of the eye-rolling and laughing his peers did in Jiro's proximity. When Jill, who was not really part of the crew, brought it up to them, they all just laughed it off. After all, everyone knew Jiro was bound to be fired as soon as the executive team realized how incompetent he really was. Although somewhat shocked that the normally quiet Jill had confronted them on this, Gary shrugged it off and fell back into the old routine with the rest of the gang.

Growing in confidence and solidarity, Gary and his teammates had recently taken to calling themselves the Marketing Mavens. The group had begun to resemble more of a high-school clique than a marketing department. They always sat together at company meetings, events, and lunch. They did things together on the weekends and went for drinks after work. If truth be told, they purposely didn't invite people outside the team more often than not. The reality was Gary spent almost no time at the office with anyone other than his beloved Mavens. He sat with them at meetings, they traveled together on business trips, and they made sure they worked on the same projects together whenever possible. Gary had even made up an excuse a couple of weeks ago so he could avoid having coffee with one of the sales directors who, frankly, was just about as annoying as Jiro.

And then one fateful December evening after work, Gary got the word he'd been waiting for. A change had been made in the marketing department and a meeting had been called for the following morning. The entire team would be present to discuss "organizational changes."

"Boom," Gary boasted as he fist bumped a teammate in a manner so quintessentially "Jiro" that they all erupted in laughter. Finally, Jiro would be gone, Gary would run the team, and life would be good. They'd work hard, play hard, and take this company to the next level.

Jiro Dreams of Sales

I look like I was poured into this suit, Jiro boasted to himself as he admired his reflection in the glass window of the meeting room he strutted past. At this point, he'd waited so long to get out of the marketing department and back to where he belonged on the sales team, Jiro could barely contain his excitement. He was so happy to be done with this chapter, Jiro had gone out the night before and bought the skinniest rock star suit he could find. He looked great. And why wouldn't he? He was finally headed back to sales and this time in a big way. *"Vice president of North American sales" has a nice ring to it*, he puffed as he thought back on his two-year journey.

When they'd initially asked him to take on the marketing role, Jiro had reluctantly accepted. He was not afraid of a challenge by any means. He had won state championship not so long ago for goodness sakes. And he knew his old college friend and colleague Junior, who ran the sales department, would owe him a favor down the road if he made this sacrifice. But still, he didn't have a love for marketing and he had no interest in managing a team—certainly not this team. But like a good soldier, he took the job and did his best in spite of it all.

From the start, it went poorly for Jiro. He just couldn't relate to his new team, and they certainly weren't fond of his management style. Admittedly, he acted more like a varsity football coach than a polished mentor, but that's all he knew. He couldn't understand why they never responded to him. But Jiro was determined to keep his eye on the prize. His ultimate goal to get back into sales kept him motivated. So when his team started to get a bit out of control—joking and laughing and even mocking him, he let it go. There were four or five of them who were really starting to get on his nerves. To be honest, he couldn't tell them apart at this point. In moments of weakness, Jiro sometimes imagined how things would have gone down back in his football days if anyone treated him the way they did. Some of the team were worse than others, but if he was honest, the only one who didn't give him problems was Jill. She wasn't the sharpest knife in the drawer, but for all her faults, Jill gave her best effort all the time and actually went out of her way to understand his perspective and ask for advice. The rest of them were all the same to him. They certainly thought they were "all that," but none of them really ever understood what he was trying to do. He knew they didn't respect him as a marketer—hell, he wasn't a marketer. But they didn't have to be so disrespectful.

Loose Lips Sink Ships

It was meeting day. There seemed to be a lot of tension in the air as everyone on the marketing team anticipated what was about to come. There had been a flurry of phone calls the night before and more than a few cocktails as the Mavens speculated about what would happen. The general consensus was Jiro must be gone. What else could it possibly be?

The team gathered in the meeting room and talked among themselves as they waited for proceedings to begin. Gary was in mid-conversation as he watched in awe as Jiro pranced by in what looked to be a five-thousand-dollar suit—and quite possibly three sizes too small. The rest of the Mavens, all witnessing the same thing, exchanged glances that gave away their confusion and concern.

What the...?

Distracted by Jiro's quarterback-like silhouette draped in Tom Ford, it was not surprising none of the team had noticed that one of their group was absent. Jill was the lone team member not yet in the room. When she finally walked into the room she was not alone.

Jill looked like a child compared to the figure next to her. Junior, a hulk of a man and the company's legendary sales vice president, stood before them ready to start the meeting. It took a minute for the Mavens to put the puzzle together.

"Hello, marketing team," boomed Junior, who looked more like a linebacker than an executive. "I'm sure you're all wondering what's going on and why your illustrious leader, Jiro, isn't here."

Please say he's fired. Please say he's fired. Gary was on the edge of his seat.

Junior continued in a voice that sounded better suited to lead a charge into battle than to run a business meeting.

"The company has decided to merge sales and marketing together. It's been in the works for a while and I'm thrilled to welcome you to my team." Gary shifted nervously in his chair as Junior delivered the bad news. "And no need to worry about our friend Jiro; he's been promoted to run our North American sales team, and we're lucky to have him back in the field."

Gary stared blankly across the room as a million worst-case scenarios flashed in his mind. *Life is so not fair. But at least Jiro will be out of our hair.* He snapped out of his trance and asked the only logical question he could think of.

"So what does that mean for our team exactly?" Gary lobbed in, as though he wanted to rip off the Band-Aid rather than draw out the pain any longer.

"Great question," Junior pointed. "When we put Jiro in charge of the team, a big part of his role was to evaluate the group and make a plan for our new merged organization." Gary visibly winced. He looked across at his friends, who, like he was, were now starting to fear that the unthinkable could have happened. "Before he left, Jiro recommend one of your very own teammates to take on the leadership role in the new and improved marketing department." Junior smiled broadly.

Oh no.

"I'm thrilled to give you our last piece of great news. I'm sure you'll all be pleased to congratulate Jill on her new promotion to director of worldwide marketing!"

Barf. Gary fought back the urge to yell out obscenities or to throw up right there on the conference room table. Instead, he applauded politely as he wondered where it had all gone wrong.

What We Can Learn From Gary

Gary's story depicts a classic mistake many of us make, especially in the early stages of our careers. The good news is it's a straightforward problem to correct. But to fix it, we have to be honest with ourselves and actually take action against it. Like many of the lessons in this book, the truth can hurt, and we have to be objective in our self-assessment. I look back on my times being a part of the herd with embarrassment and regret. The reality is it demonstrates personal weakness in all of us who have done it. On the one hand, Gary and his teammates simply weren't behaving professionally. There is no excuse for this and it still surprises me how often I see it. On the other hand, none of the Mavens understood the importance of differentiating yourself from the competition. Jiro couldn't tell them apart. They spent so much time as a group, they became indistinguishable from one another. Promotions are scarce. It can take years for the right opportunity to present itself. You must have successfully positioned yourself and your unique value if you want to win when the time comes.

Gary's plight is proof that no matter how talented you are, if you don't manage your career carefully, you won't get ahead. By contrast, following a smart career strategy can overcome many classical management weaknesses. We saw evidence of this with Jill, who was given a promotion almost by default.

The majority of managers I counsel have fallen into Gary's trap from time to time because it is so therapeutic to gripe and gossip. It's a very natural, unifying force for a team to gang up on the leader in one form or another. Never fall into this trap.

The herd mentality is the path of least resistance if we let our emotions control our career strategies. The temptation for all of us is to share our feelings and frustrations with people who are in the same boat because it makes us feel better in the short term. But was we've discussed, this is a zero-upside proposition. Your best-case scenario when you herd with your peers is that you'll feel a sense of solidarity with others experiencing the same stress as you. But that will never get you a raise or a promotion. It just makes you indistinguishable from your competitors. On the other hand, if your boss detects that you're disrespecting him or her, it could get you fired or blacklisted. Even if you're not being disrespectful, when you only spend time with peers, you're not actively building relationships with your key influencers.

Gary showed us how much more comfortable it is to build our professional relationships at our own level and below, or just within our own team. It's much harder to tactically network above our level in the company, so most of us don't do it. And worse, we often go a step further and openly criticize those who do network with their superiors. We label them as suck-ups or as political animals because we are jealous. In reality, if you're not networking vertically within your organization, you are simply not executing the optimal career strategy. The only people in a company with the power to elevate your stature are the people above your station.

Instead of hanging with his friends and talking about Jiro all day, Gary should have been building relationships and acting like a leader. That way, when change inevitably occurred, it would have been him instead of Jill who got the promotion. Gary learned the hard way that skill and talent are useless if you don't play the right career strategy.

━━━━━━

Let's take a look at the story of Larry the Loyal Guy to see how another manager approached a similar scenario. We can steal a few of his tactics for our own game plan when trying to manage herd dynamics in the workplace.

The Tale of Larry the Loyal Guy

"Does Randy Moss still play for the Vikings?" Larry belted to his wife, Jane, from across the room.

"Seriously? You're still working on that football pool for work?" she flipped back.

"Oh, never mind. I'll figure it out," Larry relinquished. He hated football with a passion. *The things I do to get ahead*, he thought as he put the finishing touches on his lineup for Sunday and refocused on the marketing plan he was multitasking.

For the better part of a year, Larry had been doing whatever it took to get into the good graces of his boss, Wilson. And from September to February, that meant the company football pool. His wife couldn't understand why he didn't just tell Wilson to shove it, but Larry knew better. It wasn't like he organized the pool; that would just be silly. But Larry was well aware that when it came to managing your career, it was the personal things that mattered in the end. He had made all the mistakes a hundred times before.

A New Coach

Wilson wasn't the worst boss in the world, Larry surmised. But pretty close. For one, he had no interest in marketing whatsoever. He almost seemed to be in the role temporarily by the way he acted on a day-to-day basis. Not a week went by when Wilson didn't reminisce publically about the good old days working with his buddies on the retail side of the company. "Marketing people just don't get it. They have no idea how it is on the front lines," he would whisper in a tone more suitable for a World War II veteran than a business executive.

Wilson had been brought across from the retail business unit nine months earlier to spearhead a new marketing department. The overarching goal for the team was to achieve better alignment between corporate marketing and the retail franchises. It certainly seemed like a noble initiative but also a little naive from Larry's point of view.

Wilson's predecessor, who the team all loved and admired, had been a true marketer through and through. He was a master of the fundamentals and he embraced a creative culture. He'd left under somewhat cloudy circumstances, but most of the team speculated he was moments away from joining Apple or Google or one of the other giants.

As soon as Wilson took over the team, controversy followed. Unlike their previous leader, Wilson was just not one of the gang. For starters he ran his meetings like Vince Lombardi and used enough football metaphors to fill up Lambeau Field several times over. It was embarrassing just to be there and witness it firsthand. Wilson also had what the team collectively coined "shiny object syndrome." He simply couldn't focus on a priority for more than a week at a time. Every subsequent priority was the most important thing in the world and the company would surely fail unless it was implemented immediately. As a result, the team became very frustrated. After only a few quarters under Wilson's command, rumblings about new jobs and swapping recruiter phone numbers began. What had started as quiet concern was quickly escalating into widespread panic.

The team had always been a closely knit group. Losing their leader had been a blow to them. They had always considered themselves to be stars and felt underappreciated at the company. From the moment Wilson took over the department, most of the group banded together in defiance of their new leader. The defiance itself started out innocently enough—positive in public but gossip and gripe in private. But as the days and weeks passed, and the team looked less and less like it did in the glory days, the defiance became more public. On a couple of occasions, it actually got quite awkward as Wilson seemed to overhear the team members making fun of him.

To his credit, Larry, who had seen managers come and go in a number of companies, didn't allow himself to react emotionally to his new boss, even though almost everything his teammates complained about was accurate. He just didn't see the value in complaining about the person in the best position to determine his future in the company. And whereas that logic seemed so obvious to Larry, it clearly escaped his less seasoned peers.

Larry decided to make a game of it. In true football spirit, he put a basic game plan together. Whenever his fellow team members started to joke and gossip about Wilson, Larry would leave the room. Whenever a peer approached him with some complaint about their boss, Larry would suggest they have a conversation with Wilson about it. It felt a little weird at first, but he knew it was the smart approach. A couple times, Larry even sensed his teammates were making fun of him too, lumping him and Wilson into the same jokes. But Larry wasn't going to let himself fall into this trap again. He'd already paid the price once before. Larry was all too aware that although griping might feel good in the moment, ultimately it never got anyone promoted.

The dysfunctional team dynamic continued for several months. A few of Larry's teammates even left the company.

Many of the others continued to display their obvious lack of respect for Wilson with low effort and constant grumbling. The team was clearly becoming a problem and everyone knew it. What once may have been an underappreciated team of stars was now just a bad team.

In private moments, the team's dialogue revolved around speculating Wilson's imminent demise. One of Larry's peers confided in him, "They must have noticed how screwed up our team is these days. There's no way they'll keep Wilson around for much longer."

"I'm not so sure," Larry counseled, conscious not to give away too much of his strategy. Then, as if he was foreshadowing what would happen next he said, "What makes you so sure they'll conclude Wilson is the problem and not us?"

Touchdown

The following Monday, Larry was summoned into Wilson's office, ostensibly to talk about the epic Vikings collapse the day before. He had scanned the sports section quickly over breakfast to make sure he could fake it when the topic of the big game inevitably arose. There had been some eye rolling from his wife at her husband's extracurricular activities.

"Our offensive line is pathetic!" Wilson shouted before Larry had even fully entered his office. "I mean seriously, we had zero pass protection in the fourth quarter." He was analyzing like the stereotypical Monday morning quarterback.

"What about all the dropped balls?" Larry threw back, trying his best not to be exposed as a football fraud.

"Exactly. Exactly." Wilson gave a look as though he had just given up on life.

Larry took a seat as the football conversation abruptly came to an end. He sensed a more serious topic of conversation was about to follow.

"Larry, I have good news and bad news," Wilson laid out. "The bad news is, they're breaking up the team and doing some restructuring. We'll be losing some people." Larry's stomach dropped. "Management feels our little experiment to try and get closer to the retail unit hasn't gone far enough. They've decided to go all the way this time."

This doesn't sound promising. Larry listened closely, not sure what was about to come next.

"So they're taking the one big team and dividing it into two: a corporate marketing team and a retail marketing team. They're hoping a dedicated retail marketing group will have the impact we've been searching for."

Uh oh.

"Management has asked me to run the retail team because that's where my experience is. They're sure I can hit the ground running." Wilson seemed pleased with his new appointment. "Now for the good news."

Give it to me. Give it to me. Give it to me. Larry held his breath as he waited for the good news.

"I've recommended you to lead the new corporate team. It will be a big increase in responsibility, but I'm sure you can handle it. I'm also pretty sure you'll be wanting to reevaluate some of the staff. Frankly, we both know they're not team players." Wilson smiled like a proud father.

Touchdown! Larry was spiking an imaginary football in his head. He'd been planning his strategy for the better part of a year, and it had finally paid off.

Your Personal Playbook: Don't Be a Part of the Herd

We learned some valuable lessons from the stories of Gary and Larry. These tales will hit home for almost everyone. Sadly, most of us fall into Gary's trap a few times before we finally get the message. Being part of the herd will get you nowhere. At best, it will make you indistinguishable from your career competitors. At worst, it can cost you your job and set your career back many years.

Gossiping and complaining about your boss or colleagues is a no-win strategy. Don't fall into this trap. If you want to get ahead in your career, take the opposite approach of the mob. When everyone else jokes and complains about the boss, you should embrace him or her. It's completely irrelevant whether you like your boss or not, or whether she's effective or smart or talented. None of that matters. The only thing that does matter is influencing the people who will control your path up the corporate ladder. Here are some can't-miss tips to make sure you never get stuck in the herd:

- Never be negative. It never pays to be negative about your colleagues or your boss. Even if you're surrounded by incompetence, you can't get anywhere by being negative. It may seem disingenuous at times, but you have to act positive at all times and about all people.

- Create an image of loyalty and respect. Find as many opportunities as you can to show deference and respect for your boss. These opportunities come up a lot if you're looking for them. Don't debate with your boss in public but look for healthy debate opportunities in private.

▶ Focus on differentiating yourself from others. Don't ever forget your peers at work are your competition. They're not your friends—at least not in the game of career management. You need to be looking for ways to elevate yourself above other people on the team. A good first step is to spend more time with your boss and less time with your teammates.

6. Find *Big* Problems to Solve

In this section, we're going to hear the stories of Randy and Harvey. Their tales touch on a very common trap managers fall into. Randy's story comes from a former employee of mine for whom I have the utmost respect. It took him a long time to realize the success he deserved. Harvey's story comes from a more recent time in my career where I sat on a multi-department strategic project team. We're going to see two contrasting approaches to career management in these stories. Randy's strategy is about reliability. Harvey's strategy is about recognition. We'll see how these two approaches ultimately led to very different results for their careers.

The Tale of Randy the Reliable

Today is the day, Randy reassured himself as he downed the last bite of his daily fiber cereal and checked his watch.

"I'll make the bed and put the laundry away, and then I've got to run and catch the 7:25 a.m. train," he instructed to his wife and high school sweetheart with a peck on the cheek.

"Okay, babe," Betty said glowingly. She knew she could always count on Randy; he was her rock.

There was a great deal of anticipation in the air this morning in Randy's household. They had been waiting for this day for what seemed like an eternity. Today was the long-awaited announcement for the newest area vice president role at Key Lime Tech. It was a position Randy had long coveted.

What About Jacobson?

As Randy made his final pre-work preparations he gave himself a much needed pep talk. *Nobody deserves this more than you,* he motivated himself in the bathroom mirror, trying his best to look the part of an executive. He did deserve it. He'd been with the company for the better part of four years, and in the mobile development business, that actually meant something. Randy was well respected in the office, and for the most part his colleagues and peers admired him, much like Betty did. Randy really was a rock.

But as much as Randy knew he deserved the promotion, he also knew it was not a foregone conclusion. There were certainly no guarantees in this business. Randy had learned this the hard way six months earlier when he'd been passed over for the last VP vacancy. At the time, he had been quite sure it was his for the taking.

"That one was just bad luck," Randy reminisced with Yves, his friend and colleague whom he sat with on the train into work every morning.

"Totally. I mean, what were the chances Jessica would have created that new sales compensation program just as the promotions were in play?" Like Betty, Yves was one of Randy's biggest fans.

"I didn't even know the old program was a problem," Randy agreed helplessly. "Except for that silly Jacobson thing, I've hit my numbers, my projects have been on time, and our process is running as smoothly as ever. If they can't see the quality of the work I'm doing, that's their problem."

"Nobody remembers Jacobson," Yves consoled him with a white lie.

"One thing is for sure: My house is in order now!" Randy mentally doubled down with an almost-imperceptible hint of doubt in his voice.

They continued on to the office with Randy reassuring himself along the way that his hard work and efforts would be recognized and the long-awaited promotion would soon be his.

Caught Between a Rock and a...

The hiring and orientation committee at Key Lime Tech was made up of seven executives and two human resources leaders. The group met every second Tuesday with the directive of ensuring all new employees were properly indoctrinated into the company, as well as to make certain they met the organization's three tenets of excellence: innovation, empathy, and inspiration—"I.E.I." Or, as the staff had come to call it, "aaaayy eeeeeee aaaayy"—always with a wincing look on their faces as they said it.

As much as the staff joked about the three tenets, the management team seemed to take them quite seriously. More than one talented candidate had been passed over for not demonstrating these cultural virtues. In addition to hiring and orienting new staff members, the committee also weighed in on promotions and role changes. That was the purpose of their meeting today.

The committee's chairman, Troy Tapp, kicked off the meeting. "Today we'll review the area vice president vacancy," he instructed. "We've got Allison and Randy up for consideration, so let's hear from the affected parties." He pointed specifically at the committee representatives from the sales department as he said it.

"Randy has been here the longest and his work is top notch. No brainer for me," declared Randy's direct manager and friend, Eric.

"I agree Randy's work is solid and people seem to like him. But is he really leadership material?" questioned Martha, a director from the services department who was clearly working a different agenda. "Sure, he'll get the job done, but has he really ever done anything great?" Several nods were exchanged around the conference room table as Martha's point seemed to hit the mark. "Come to think of it, the only time I have heard Randy's name in the last year was that procurement snafu that cost us the Jacobson deal. Is that what we want to bank our future on?"

"What about Allison?" suggested Jasmine, the human resources vice president and co-chair of the council. "I know she helped right the ship after the Jacobson deal, and I heard she was a big part of implementing Jessica's sales compensation plan. I'm not sure she's as consistent as Randy or even as experienced but it seems like everything she touches helps advance the ball for the company. We could use more of that."

"Hang on a minute," Eric cautioned with his hands pressed together in front of his face. "Allison can be a bit unpredictable and her forecasting can be very dicey sometimes. Don't we want someone we can count on?"

The committee debated back and forth between the two candidates for the better part of an hour. Randy, whose reputation for being a solid performer was well documented—minus that one Jacobson blemish—was a pretty safe choice. None of the committee members could debate that. Allison on the other hand, though less consistent, had several big wins to her credit—although it wasn't entirely clear the role she'd played in all of those projects. It was a tough decision facing the group that day, but in the end they made the call.

Always the Bridesmaid

As Randy walked toward the meeting room, he checked his watch to make sure he wasn't too early. He was conscious of looking overly eager in his big moment. He deliberately slowed his pace and took a deep breath. *I've worked so hard for this.* Randy had kept his head down and his work was solid. He'd put in his time and he hadn't made a single mistake since Jacobson. *I need this*, he thought to himself as he entered the meeting room.

"Good afternoon, Randy," welcomed Jasmine with an outstretched arm.

"Hi, Jasmine," Randy responded while trying to gauge her demeanor.

"I want you to know that we really appreciate the work you do here. You're one of our most reliable managers and you're a vital part of our company," she flattered him almost apologetically.

Oh god. Not again. Randy's heart sunk as he got that familiar feeling.

"I'm sorry to tell you we've decided to award the new area vice president role to Allison."

"No!" Randy blurted out before he could control himself.

"I'm sorry, Randy. I know you must feel disappointed but I'm sure you can agree Allison is a strong problem-solver and more than capable of doing the job. We'll need to rely on you pretty heavily to help her get up to speed in the new region. I hope we can count on you as always."

Randy wanted to scream. How could he have been passed over yet again? He was a rock. People could count on him. He almost never made mistakes. It all seemed so unfair.

"But..." Randy stopped himself. "Yes, I'm sure Allison will be great and I'm happy to help in any way I can," he managed to conclude like a true professional.

Now what am I supposed to do?

What We Can Learn From Randy

I've seen a lot of Randys in my career. They are one of the most tragic characters in an organization, and they deserve so much more than they get. If reliability and consistency were the stepping-stones to success they would be at the top. Randy was dependable, smart, and hardworking. He almost never made mistakes with tasks assigned to him, but it wasn't enough. It almost never is.

The moral of Randy's story is that being reliable is just not enough to advance your career. At least not to the executive level. Reliability is a passive career-management strategy that will not bring you the visibility required to make it to the top. Contrary to conventional logic, a career strategy based on consistency and small victories is actually higher risk than one based on big wins and major projects. Many of us like to think we will be noticed for consistently solid work. But in practice, consistency is only enough to provide career security. Career advancement demands more.

A lack of big, visible wins is ultimately what led to Randy's lack of progress. It had two material impacts on his would-be promotion. First, it meant influential people didn't hear about him enough. He just wasn't visible and certainly hadn't created an image as someone ready for leadership. Secondly, because he had no big wins, his mistakes were amplified. Without clear victories to counter his losses, Randy only became known for his one big mistake—the Jacobson deal. Allison, on the other hand, seemingly had many mistakes under her belt, and was less competent on a day-to-day basis. But when it came to promotion time, she was remembered for the few big wins and not the many small mistakes she made along the way.

To advance your career you have to put points up on the board. Points, in your career, like in football or rugby, come in a couple of varieties. Consistently delivering against your responsibilities and doing solid work in your day-to-day tasks wins you lots of small points. We'll call them career field goals. And if you never make any mistakes, those points accumulate over time—slowly. On the flip side, when you inevitably do make mistakes you lose points, too. The problem is, in my experience, one career mistake is worth at least five career field goals. So it can be a challenge even for very reliable people like Randy to build up enough points using the field goal strategy to put a winning score up on the board in the end.

On the other hand, recognition for being associated with a big project gets you big points. We'll call them career touchdowns. If you're actively looking for them, you'll see that opportunities for career touchdowns present themselves all the time. They often don't directly impact your personal objectives, and it will frequently look like there isn't much to gain from all the extra work you'll have to do by taking them on. You should do it anyway. Because like in football and rugby, even if you score a lot of field goals, your opponent is always only one or two touchdowns away from catching or surpassing you.

An effective career strategy has to be about scoring touchdowns. It's about big plays and projects. Though playing a safe, consistent game will keep you employed and keep your boss happy, it's an extremely difficult strategy to actually win with. As we saw with Allison and Jessica before her, a less-competent opponent can beat you with a few lucky touchdowns even if you're more reliable on a day-to-day basis.

To break from the metaphor for a moment, the only people who are paying attention to the quality of your daily work are your direct teammates and your boss. This is almost never enough to get you a promotion—at least not after you've reached a senior management level in your career. To get promoted you need recognition outside of your direct circle of influence. Mistakes, by contrast, have a tendency to reverberate across an organization. Nobody will ever notice the 20 times you get the process right, but the one time you mess it up, it will seem as though the entire company has been affected.

So what does this mean for your strategy? It starts with changing your personal career scorecard. Stop focusing on the consistency of your daily work as the number-one priority and start seeking out opportunities to participate in big projects. The field goal strategy will not get you to the top of the company. With this in mind, the next challenge is how to find those big projects or problems that can score you the touchdowns you need to advance your career in a meaningful way.

Opportunities for career touchdowns come in two forms: Transformational Projects and Crisis Resolutions. Transformational Projects are very high risk and should be approached with some caution. Though you can score major points by spearheading a major process or concept transformation, it can also backfire on you if you violate our rule about playing with too much passion. The penalty for failing in the Transformational Project scenario is probably worth five touchdowns. So you need to be very selective about the projects you pursue. I recommend participating in, versus leading, a Transformational Project; you still score the big points, but the risk of failure is much lower. It's like being on the winning team but never seeing the field. You still get the championship ring, but you have no risk of being the scape goat for failure.

The second type of touchdown is the Crisis Resolution. Crisis Resolutions are opportunities to score points by fixing other people's mistakes. It's kind of like returning a fumble for a touchdown. This is a much safer type of career touchdown, although it won't score quite as many points. The most important thing to be cautious of is never to frame a resolution as repairing someone else's error. Alienating people or laying blame doesn't advance your career. It only creates one less person or group that will support your rise through the company.

Because mistakes are so broadly felt within a company, the recognition you can get from helping to fix it is so great it's not necessary to point fingers or lay blame. And you almost always want to give some credit, deserved or not, to whoever created the problem in the first place to bring him or her onside. Crisis resolutions, when approached in an ultra-positive way, can have the impact of scoring you points without hurting your relationships within the organization. The best managers and executives are always helpful. They are looking for these crises to swoop in and save the day.

The moral of the story is to build your career by scoring touchdowns instead of field goals. You need to reprioritize your personal scorecard so you focus your time and energy on projects and initiatives that can actually put up enough points to beat your competitors.

The Tale of Harvey the Home Run Hitter

Harvey was late. Again. But you wouldn't know it by the look of him that Monday morning. In fact if you did look at him you'd probably see some faded remnant of the words "Red" and "Sox" mostly cleaned off his left and right cheeks. *Permanent marker—bad idea*, he half chuckled, like a man resigned to his fate. Nothing could get him down this morning. His beloved Sox had clinched the Division title and he had been there to witness it. What a party it had been.

Stuck in a Pickle

As epic as the game had been, Harvey was now late for work and he hadn't completed most of his weekly reports. You might think this was an isolated October phenomenon for our friend and Red Sox fanatic. And sometimes he tried to pretend that was the case, but there was always something: a tough four-game stint with the Yankees, a critical road series in Toronto, a must-win in Baltimore. For 162 games and about eight months of the year, Harvey was in a state of constant distraction.

Unfortunately for Harvey, though his baseball obsession was a lot of fun, it made performing well at work that much more difficult. Harvey, when not wearing his white and red uniform, was a mild-mannered product manager at Centrolink, a regional Internet service provider. And whether he was recovering from a Fenway weekend hangover or staying up late to watch his team play road games on the West Coast, Harvey regularly struggled to find the time to get his work done. But like his beloved ball club, Harvey was resourceful, and had long ago learned a valuable lesson in managing his career. Harvey was a long ball hitter.

Like all great sluggers, Harvey always looked for the right pitch. While the other managers in his department stressed out about every little daily task, Harvey prioritized the big stuff—and he sought it out, too. He was surprised how frequently his teammates actually turned down opportunities to help out on a multi-department project or a tiger team. They were always too busy. For Harvey it was a green light every time—like Red Sox speedster Jacoby Ellsbury. In fact, he recently volunteered for the Next Generation Product Committee despite the fact it meant he'd have to sacrifice his regular workload. Frankly, it was more fun to get involved in big projects and you never knew who you were going to meet.

As Harvey made the walk of shame across the office late that morning, with more than a little paint still on his face, he easily shook off the jibes flung at him by his coworkers.

"You know you're late again, don't you?" Andrea said with quite a bit of fake disappointment on her face.

"Your margin report is overdue," complained Mikey, the new guy. Harvey was pretty sure he was a closeted Blue Jays fan.

But Harvey was tough, like his hero, former Red Sox catcher Jason Varitek. So he refused to let the comments get to him. Although his colleagues thought he was lazy and a little naive, they were underestimating him. *Yankees, all of them*, he giggled to himself as he vowed not to be late again for a while.

Who's Keeping Score?

What Harvey's peers didn't understand is that, while they spent their days banging out pricing sheets and profitability reports and product requirements, he had bigger plans—"Big Papi" plans, as Harvey liked to call them. So he spent the rest of the morning catching up on his reports and other routine work so he could get back to his master plan and be done in time to watch the game.

"They should just fire him," Andrea gossiped with a pointed finger from across the room. "He barely gets his work done and he's late all the time. I haven't been late in a year and nobody even seems to notice." She was whining now and feeling sorry for herself.

"He's not that bad," said Mikey, showing a special sort of selective memory reserved for Toronto Blue Jays fans. "I mean, he did launch the new product delivery process and he is on the Next Gen Product Committee. That's not nothing."

"Sure, but when's the last time he handed in his reports on time?" Andrea fired back, obviously not realizing she was one of the few people who actually cared about that.

This was the perpetual debate within the product management team: whether Harvey's big contributions made up for his poor work ethic and inconsistent effort on the routine tasks. But for the most part nobody outside of their little department was aware of the debate at all. And little did they know, but they would all find out the answer to their question much sooner than they thought.

#HOMERUN

"Where the heck is Harvey now?" Andrea complained as though he'd stolen her favorite fuzzy head pencil.

There had been a last-minute meeting called by their team's manager, and everyone but Harvey had rushed to make it on time. But as she slowed her jog in front of the glass meeting room wall, Andrea got her answer. She was startled to see her nemesis, Harvey, already in the room—small-talking with their general manager, who was visiting from out of town.

Andrea pulled out her smartphone and watched the exchange in disgust.

"Sure, Jeter can get on base, but he has no power to the gaps anymore." Amanda entered mid-sentence as Harvey parried with the GM.

"Harvey, Harvey, Harvey, I see you're a lost cause," he patted him on the back like old friends. "We'll have to get you out to a game when the Sox come to New York—see if we can't bring you back from the dark side."

#wtf?!?! Andrea texted to Mikey, who had clearly witnessed the same exchange across the table.

When the team was all seated, they waited anxiously for the GM to start the meeting.

"Hey, guys. Sorry for the last-minute stuff," he apologized, as though it was the one hundredth time he'd asked for forgiveness for the same thing. "We're here today to say goodbye to one of our brethren."

Andrea's eyes opened like saucers as she mouthed "Wow" across the table to her buddy.

"We're saying goodbye to Harvey today. He's been a big part of this team for a while now and I'm sure you're all sorry to see him go." He said it with hands open and directed at Harvey.

#justice!!!! Andrea typed when she should have been clapping respectfully like the rest of the team.

"But," the GM wasn't finished. A lump started to form in Andrea's throat. "Our loss is the strategic alliances team's gain," he continued on proudly after quite a long pause for dramatic effect. "Harvey has been asked to head up a brand-new team to develop new strategic partnerships for our company. Give a round of applause for our newest vice president of alliances!"

#killme Andrea typed without looking.

"I had the chance to work with Harvey on the Next Gen Product Committee and we all know about the great work he did on the new product delivery process. He impressed a lot of the management team and was an obvious choice for the new role."

Andrea couldn't bear to look across the table.

The GM shook Harvey's hand one more time and left the room. In true Red Sox fashion, Harvey was prepared to be graceful in victory. He politely accepted the congratulations that came from most of his colleagues. He was in a daze at all his good fortune.

What a day. Now if we can just win the World Series.

Your Personal Playbook: Find *Big* Problems to Solve

We learned a lot from the stories of Randy and Harvey. Many of you will have had similar experiences in your own career—watching people get promoted while you sit around waiting to be noticed. Randy teaches us that reliability doesn't equate to advancement. Security maybe, but not advancement. Harvey showed us how taking on big projects can erase our mistakes and make us visible to the influencers in the organization who have the power to move us up the corporate ladder. Here are a few quick tips you can use to make sure you stay focused on a touchdown strategy for your career:

- Don't wait to be noticed. Nobody is watching you. Reliability is not a leadership quality. At least not one anybody cares enough about to promote you. The best way to get to the top is to make yourself more visible by taking on bigger projects. Even if that means you volunteer for projects that have nothing to do with your objectives.

- Wait for the right pitch. You can't just swing blindly for every big project that comes your way. You need to choose the ones with the highest probability for success. The ones that will connect you to your career influencers. Having a big project failure is as profoundly bad as having a big project success is good.

- Swing for the fences. Don't turn down chances to hit a home run. They come around more than we think sometimes. Next time someone asks you to be a part of a project or to take something on outside of your objectives, say yes.

7. Don't Hold People Accountable

In this section we're going to hear the stories of Dottie and Harry. These tales address a scenario that is not as widespread as some of the others we've seen, but it can be equally deadly to your career if you're not careful. Dottie's story comes from the career of someone I've followed for many years. A person with exceptional natural talent and energy. Her story illustrates a mistake most often made by Task Masters and other highly motivated but shortsighted managers. Harry's story comes from a former colleague of mine who taught me some valuable lessons about the power of visible mentoring. We'll see how creating a perception as a mentor can be more powerful than building a reputation for driving accountability.

The Tale of Dottie the Dominatrix

"Oh no, no, no. Just no," Dottie mumbled to herself as she tilted her head to the side to get a full view of the outfit standing in front of her. *We're definitely not in Kansas anymore. Or maybe we are.* Dottie giggled on the inside as she resisted the urge to Instagram the bedazzled cowgirl number to share with her former colleagues and friends. *I'd better get to work.*

For Dottie, "work" was not an accurate description of what she did each and every day. Her work was her passion. Dottie was a fashion expert. Well, she used to be. It had been a month already and yet there were still plenty of moments when Dottie forgot where she was. And more than a few moments when she wondered if she'd made the right decision coming to work at Lydia's Leathers.

Everything Old Is New Again

Dottie's entire career up until a month ago had been spent in the fashion business—fashion editorial, to be precise. And Dottie was always precise. You had to be as a fashion editor. There were deadlines to meet and pundits to please. A lack of precision meant a lack of credibility, which was a career death sentence where she came from. You held yourself accountable and you held everyone around you to the same high standard. And if you couldn't cut it, the business chewed you up and spit you out. That's just how it was. After almost 10 years, Dottie was a pro.

After a decade in the fashion trenches Dottie had been ready for a change. After careful consideration, she had made the move out of editorial and over to retail. She joined Lydia's as an online channel manager, with responsibility for the company's Web presence. On the surface, this transition might seem quite natural, but Dottie was beginning to appreciate some fundamental differences.

Lydia's Leathers was a well-known brand from yesteryear trying to make a resurgence. A 50-year-old company with a long history behind it. Although from Dottie's perspective, its best days had long since passed. As she walked down the hall toward her office that morning, Dottie had to reassure herself it had been the right decision. *Patience, Dottie.* That was her mantra these days. She always knew it would be a big change and she had to stay positive. After all, if Dottie could bring Lydia's back to life it would be a massive achievement.

Fashion Faux Pas

A confident Dottie sat down at her desk, which she had strategically positioned to overlook her team. As she sipped her blueberry tea, the first thought that crossed her mind was, *Oh, god. What are they wearing?* It still shocked Dottie how a company in the business of outfitting consumers seemed to universally disregard even the most basic principles of fashion. *All in good time,* she recited as though it were a meditative chant of some kind.

It was time for Dottie to put her head down and get to work. The entire department was preparing for the year-end meeting, where each of the managers would present their plans for the following year. Dottie's number-one priority was to produce an impressive plan. Lydia's needed a fresh look and strategy, and she was going to do her part. Her plan would be ambitious to say the least.

One aspect of her new role that reminded Dottie of the fashion editorial business was the number of group projects required. It was a necessary evil wherever you worked, she surmised. In this case, Dottie's plan required input and contribution from three brand managers, a designer, and the merchandising VP. Further complicating matters for Dottie, none of these people technically worked for her. Though you wouldn't have known it had you been a fly on the wall that day.

A series of prep meetings was scheduled to make it easier for the managers to collaborate on their respective plans. The company's main conference room had been transformed into something more resembling the NASA command center than a meeting area. The walls were laden with a collage of images, messages, and merchandise samples. The "war room," as it was lovingly coined, would be their home for the next 30 days.

To kick off the planning process, each manager would present their basic plan structures and submit requests for contribution from their peers. It was not possible to build a plan without help from the other functional managers. Dottie was no stranger to this type of matrix environment, and felt very comfortable assigning tasks and managing others to complete them.

The first few plans were presented and Dottie was assigned a handful of simple tasks. For the most part the plans were unimpressive to her, but she reminded herself to stay focused on her own work as much as she could.

It was Dottie's turn to present. She had fully anticipated some reservations from her coworkers when she delivered her requirements. The sheer volume of preparation she was demanding would be quite a change for most of the group, who had been with the company for many years. But ultimately if they were going to be successful, everyone needed to raise their game. Dottie wouldn't accept anything less than the best. But the response she got was alarming.

"You want me to do *what?*" asked the designer.

"*How* many different looks do you want me to put together?" questioned the stylist.

"This isn't how we normally do our plans, Dottie," one of her other peers tried to reason politely.

But Dottie was determined. Her reputation was at stake. She needed a good plan. She'd been hired to make an impact. The team would have to get on board or get off the boat.

"Guys, we need to raise our game," Dottie implored them. "The old way isn't working. We haven't been taken seriously in almost a decade, and if we don't change our image we're never going to be great." Dottie needed them to understand.

Although uneasy, her fellow managers did their best to be cordial to their new colleague, not wanting to cause unnecessary conflict so soon. Some quiet nods were exchanged and they quickly moved on to the next presentation.

Afterward, in private, more than one of the other managers had comments on Dottie's demeanor. Who was she to march in, 30 days new, and start demanding all these changes and doling out all this work? It wasn't fair. And who said they weren't being taken seriously?

Closet Aggravator

A week had passed and the contributions from each manager slowly started to trickle in. Dottie was immediately alarmed by how poor the work was overall. Some of the group hadn't even completed their tasks on time, which was unheard of where Dottie had come from. And for those who had prepared, most seemed to be operating with concepts, processes, and ideas from several decades ago.

It's like they've been preserved in a hyperbaric chamber since 1987, she thought to herself as she reviewed the work. The messages were outdated. The visuals were unattractive. The marketing techniques were archaic, and the fashion designs were appalling. Dottie was mortified at what she was seeing. And those were the people who actually completed their work. It seemed to Dottie as though nobody had any passion for the work or for making the company better. *What have I gotten myself into?*

In the second war room meeting Dottie managed to hold her tongue for a while. She sat quietly and made notes on her colleagues' submissions, trying to do her best to be a model corporate citizen. However, if anyone in the room had glanced at what she was writing, they would have seen "Kill me now!" written 25 times across the yellow legal pad in front of Dottie. But when the third presenter began Dottie just couldn't contain herself any longer.

The presentation focused on the importance of using the term "genuine leather" in all brand correspondence, advertising, and promotion. It would have a major impact on every manager's plan because it was a fundamental brand component.

"Can someone explain why we think 'genuine' is such a strong message for us?" she asked rather productively. "I mean, don't people just assume our leather is genuine? We are a leather company, after all. We should be going with something more compelling like 'American-made' or 'handcrafted' or something fashion-forward that could help us break away from our history."

"Break away?" the brand manager questioned. "Why would we want to break away from 50 years of tradition?

"Well, it's clearly not working," Dottie replied indignantly. It was becoming obvious to everyone that the newest member of the company did not approve of what she was seeing. "Guys, I can't present a plan based on these designs and messages. I need you to go back and rework this stuff. We need something great, and this is definitely not great." Dottie was getting frustrated. Her plan depended on these people.

"Dottie, I'm sorry, but we've been doing it this way for half a century," one of the other managers responded.

"That's pretty obvious," Dottie said sarcastically, with an eye roll that was seen by everyone.

"Dottie, we have to say it's 'genuine leather,' for when it gets put in the discount bin in the stores, people wonder," the merchandising manager said a little too proudly.

"Well, maybe if we had some new and interesting designs we wouldn't end up in the discount bin," Dottie fired back, knowing she was right and not caring much who she offended at this point. "I mean, look at this little ivory number for winter.

What is this? 'Snowmobile chic'?" she exclaimed with more than a healthy dose of condescension in her voice. "I'm sorry, but I won't present these. You guys committed to making this plan great, and I need you to take some personal accountability here."

The rest of the meeting continued with more of the same. Dottie seemed to take on each subsequent manager on every topic under the sun—messaging, fashion designs, promotions, Website, copywriting, and on and on. In her heart she knew she was being very tough on them, but she also knew without a shadow of a doubt she was right on virtually every point. It just wasn't fair that she had to depend on such incompetent people for vital parts to her plan. It was her name on the line, after all.

The Final Thread

With only one week left before she'd have to deliver her plan, things were not looking good for Dottie. She was running out of options at this point. Virtually none of the submissions by her peers were good enough to be considered even passable by her standards. There was only one thing left she could do.

"I have to spell it out for them or they won't get it," she had told her husband that night at dinner. "They need to feel a sense of urgency or they'll never produce what we need. I need to shake things up."

And that's exactly what she did.

Dottie drafted an essay-length e-mail detailing every task required by her fellow managers to get the plan completed. She listed everything. She sent it to everyone. Dottie had come to the realization that if she wanted results she'd have to pull out the big guns. She decided to copy her boss and the superiors of each manager who had a task in her plan. *That oughtta do it,* she resolved, and finished making her plans for the next day's meeting.

It was Wednesday, which meant plan review day for Dottie and her peers. The previous meetings had been so contentious there was a palpable tension in the office that morning. Even Dottie sensed it. But tension was a feeling she had been growing increasingly comfortable with lately. It honestly felt like Dottie against the world for the past two months. She was starting to wonder if she would ever whip the team into shape.

Dottie glanced at her watch. It was time to head over to the conference room. She certainly didn't want to be late and risk setting a bad example for the very people she was trying to make over. But just as she started for the door, Louise, the company's head of HR poked her head in.

"Good morning, Dottie," she said rather seriously.

"Louise?" Dottie responded curiously. "What brings you by?"

"Why don't we take a seat?" she suggested, entering the room without waiting for an answer.

What is this about? Dottie wondered. She hadn't see Louise since the day she was hired.

"Dottie, I'm sorry to say we've been getting a lot of complaints about your attitude and inability to work in a team environment. It seems you've upset several of your colleagues." Louise looked very somber.

"Come on. Seriously?"

"I'm very serious, Dottie. And you know how important our culture is at Lydia's. It's the secret to our success."

Yeah, maybe 20 years ago. Dottie shot back using her inside voice, "Okay. So what exactly is the issue?"

"I'm afraid we've had several complaints that you're creating conflict. You're speaking harshly to your peers and you're generally making others around you feel uncomfortable. That is not the way we do things at Lydia's."

"Well, I'm sorry, but I was brought here to make changes, and to freshen up our offerings and brand. If I've ruffled a few feathers along the way, isn't that the price of change?"

Louise shook her head. "Dottie, I need you to adjust your tone and your approach to working with your peers. We can't have a negative work environment. It's not the Lydia's way."

Louise handed Dottie a document. "This is a performance improvement plan. We're giving you 30 days to improve your attitude and the way you interact with your colleagues."

"Okay," Dottie was getting nervous and pissed off at the same time.

"If, at the end of the 30-day period, you have improved, we can all go on working together happily. But if we haven't seen measureable improvement and great feedback from your peers, we will have to explore options that involve you moving on from the company."

"Okay, Louise. I understand." What else could she say?

As soon as Louise left the room Dottie put her head in her hands. *Did this just happen?* She was bewildered. *I'm trying to do the right things, do great work, get people to raise their games, and now* I'm *on a P.I.P. How on earth did I end up here?*

What We Can Learn From Dottie

Dottie shows us another example of why talent and expertise alone will not advance your career. In fact, they can send your career into a tailspin if you don't apply them correctly. For smart managers like Dottie, it can be very hard to accept this fact. You'll often hear them defend their actions by pointing to the accuracy and validity of their perspectives. They are missing the most important point. Your career isn't played in a vacuum. Being successful in a corporation requires you play the correct strategy based on your environment. Dottie failed to assess her playing field.

Most corporate cultures reject conflict. As managers, we know we should embrace healthy conflict, but in practice we do not. Most people fight against accountability. Especially being held accountable by peers. But instead of working with her environment, Dottie fought against it—and lost. Nine times out of 10, a strategy based on demanding accountability is not the optimal approach to advance your career.

Accountability has been a business best practice for a long time now and holding people accountable is a universal must-do in management circles. We've been taught how critical it is to drive a team to perform, to demand personal accountability and excellence from your team and peers. Though this sounds great in theory, I don't believe it to be true in practice. When you hold people accountable you illicit an instinctively defensive response as people's personal objectives always take precedence over corporate objectives.

When it comes to doling out accountability, there two scenarios worth mentioning. The first is holding your employees accountable. Because they report to us, we can hold our staff accountable to a certain extent. But even in this scenario, I have had much greater success helping versus holding accountable. For our purposes, let's focus on the second scenario, which is where most managers get into trouble. The second scenario is holding your peers accountable. In my opinion, this is a career-limiting strategy for most of us. For starters, you do not have legitimate power over your peers. You can't force them to be accountable unless they acquiesce—and you can't fire them. In a perfect world all your peers do what is best for the company. They are all open to criticism and feedback. They demand accountability of themselves and others. But that is not the world you're playing in.

In the real world, your peers will never do what's best for the company when it's at odds with what is best for them personally—nor should they. So when you are tough on them or hold them accountable for work quality or deadlines, you take on very limited upside proposition. You can't actually win much of anything by holding people accountable. The best possible outcome is they deliver what was expected in the first place and you may benefit in some small way as a result. But the downside potential is much more devastating. You can lose allies in the organization. You can alienate yourself. You can be perceived as disruptive or difficult. These are much harder to bounce back from than a delayed project or low-quality output.

We saw Dottie make the mistake of assuming her peers viewed the situation through the same lens she did. She assumed they wanted to shake things up at Lydia's as much as she did. But of course they didn't. Most of her peers had been with the company for a decade or more. They built all the messages and designs she was criticizing. To support Dottie would be to condemn themselves. Human beings won't do that. Dottie paid a big price for blindly holding her peers accountable without contemplating the larger game at play.

Instead of holding people accountable I recommend helping them. Mentoring and support for your weaker peers is a great way to accomplish two objectives simultaneously. First, if you offer your help sincerely you can often get your project or issue back on track anyway. Pushing people is rarely the fastest way to getting the output you want. Demonstrating empathy is a much stronger play. Second, if you demonstrate your help and support to key influencers, you build an image of leadership that is vital to your career advancement. When people see you helping your peers, it positions you above them in the minds of others. Helping your peers is a win-win for you.

━━━━━

Doling out accountability is a move for the herd. Leadership by helping people is what can separate you from your peers and accelerate your career. Let's look at the story of Harry the Helper for a great example of how a helping strategy can be effective.

The Tale of Harry the Helper

The parking lot at IglooTech was full. It was five minutes after nine and most of the staff had been at work for half an hour at least. Harry slammed the driver's-side door to his aging Toyota Tercel and waddled as quickly as he could toward the building's front entrance. *This is the year I start jogging,* he lied to himself as he entered the office. Tardiness was not uncommon for Harry. And normally he wouldn't have given it a second thought, but today was different. It was Friday, which meant the entire engineering team held their "stand-up" session. During this weekly fixture the functional managers shared the work they'd done in the latest software development sprint.

Harry managed the user experience team at IglooTech and had been in the role for about a year. As he made his way into the building, he reflected on his tenure thus far in the department. It had been many years since he had been on a team as big as this one. Having spent the lion's share of his career working in technical support, he wasn't used to having so many management peers to work alongside. Now, as a member of the engineering department, he had five management peers: architecture, core engineering, application development, infrastructure, and quality assurance. Each group had many staff and important contributions to the product. The unique challenge of working with so many fellow managers was that each depended on the other to make the whole product function. It could be a stressful environment for some as they collectively struggled to influence their peers without legitimate authority over them.

Outside the Box

When he accepted the new role, Harry knew there would be challenges, but felt his experience supporting customers might be an advantage for him. He held a unique view of the product that many engineering insiders did not have. In his previous role, he had sat through hundreds of hours of customer support calls. He knew better than most how the product was actually used in practice, and when it came to handing crisis situations, Harry was a pro.

The majority of people in the engineering department found their motivation in the work itself. They were genuinely passionate about coding and the software development process. Harry was not one of them. Frankly, he was not the best coder or even the best manager. There were times Harry felt his management peers looked down on him because he wasn't born and bred a programmer. But he knew in his heart he had value to add. He was a bigger-picture thinker and longed for the opportunity to have more influence on the strategic direction of the product line.

"Maybe I'm not the best coder in the world and maybe I can't tell a controller from a compiler. But I know our product and I know our customers, and that has to count for something!" He had pleaded to his wife unnecessarily that morning. She, of course, was always on his side.

Harry shuffled as fast as he could toward the meeting area. You didn't want to be late to a stand-up session for several reasons. Not the least of which was that you'd miss out on the delicious maple donuts one of the quality assurance engineers brought in each week. A stand-up without donuts was unthinkable. Of slightly less importance to Harry, the stand-up was also the time when the group managers got to demonstrate their progress. To say there was healthy competition among the peers would be a mild understatement. As he raced to the conference table to find an empty donut box waiting for him, Harry was more determined than ever to prove his worth on the team. Today he would show his boss and everyone else he was a force to be reckoned with.

Stand-Up Stand-Up

Tracy Matthews was vice president of engineering and Harry's boss at IglooTech. As she sat in her office making final preparations for the stand-up session she gazed around the meeting area. *What a team I've assembled*, she thought to herself as she polished off her second maple donut of the morning.

Phase one of her plan had come together nicely. She finally had all the functional groups in place with strong managers overseeing each one. Tracy had fought hard a year earlier to move the company to an Agile development process, against the recommendation of several of the old guard. It's not like it was a completely radical change, but for a company that had done it one way for so many years it certainly shook things up. But now, after nine months of constant change, the team was looking pretty good.

To be fair, the transition had not been uneventful. The team had experienced some hiccups, as they were now moving so much faster than before. The biggest challenge they faced was with product integration—fitting all the pieces together from each of the teams. But for Tracy these hurdles were expected. First they had to learn to move fast; now they'd learn to work synergistically.

Commence phase two of the master plan, Tracy thought. Phase two for Tracy was to unify the groups under one engineering director who would be responsible for making sure the groups worked in sync. This would resolve the integration challenges they had been facing and result in a higher-quality end product. For the past few weeks she had been observing her six managers in hopes of being able to select one of them to take on the director role as soon as possible.

It had been easy for Tracy to narrow the list down to three. The others were just not ready for that level of responsibility yet. When she assessed her managers objectively, three were very strong and three were still learning.

The frontrunner for the director position was Lisa, a 20-year coding wizard and a bit of a company icon. Lisa was revered for her notorious coding binges, which could go for

24 hours or more. A close second was Brent, a meticulous C++ engineer. Brent demanded precision from himself and his team at all times. He was an extremely efficient developer, but could be a bit hard on his peers and staff. And then there was Harry, a dark horse to be sure, but someone Tracy had kept her eye on for a while. What he lacked as a developer he made up for in other ways. He had a knack for bringing out the best in people and for solving difficult problems in unconventional ways. *We'll see how this stand-up goes*, Tracy thought to herself, with every intention of making the decision later that same day.

It was weekly stand-up time and the engineering team gathered together with all but Harry feeling quite satisfied from their fill of maple donuts. The format for the stand-up was intended to be highly collaborative. Each manager would take a turn presenting his progress, and the group would ask questions and discuss integration ideas and challenges. Soon after the presentations began a pattern started to emerge.

First up had been Lisa, who looked like she was on the tail end of a marathon coding session. She wowed the group with her innovative approach to the latest version of the core engine. Many of the team were shocked by the sheer volume of code she had written since they had last met. Lisa's legendary status seemed to grow every week. If there had been a vote for team MVP, Lisa would have won every time. However, as strong as her presentation was, Lisa did not handle collaboration well. A couple of times when members of the team asked questions about how or why she implemented aspects of her work, she frankly seemed unwilling or uninterested in sharing. It was as though she had a secret she preferred to keep to herself.

Brent was next, and as always, he demonstrated extremely clean code from his group. All were impressed by the thought and precision that went into their work. The team looked up to Brent as a pure-bred programmer who did everything right. His work was always tested, documented, and altogether solid. But like Lisa, Brent struggled when it came to accepting other ideas and feedback. When one of the other managers offered an alternative approach to solving the problem, Brent barked a list of reasons why it was a silly suggestion. On a couple of occasions he responded in a way that seemed more designed to shut a teammate down than provide an explanation.

The third presenter was Harry. His presentation went without much fanfare. It didn't have the awe factor of Lisa's or the efficiency of Brent's. But overall the work was solid. What was very apparent to everyone was how heavily he seemed to rely on his team to explain the code and rationale behind it. In fact, Harry only did about 25 percent of the presenting and had his team do the rest. A couple of times it actually seemed like he didn't fully grasp some of the more sophisticated concepts his team was putting forth. If was a very different presentation, to say the least. But it wasn't his presentation that made Tracy take notice of him. It was what happened next.

The remaining three presentations were led by the weaker group managers—the ones not being considered by Tracy for promotion. In this kind of fast-paced environment you were only as strong as your weakest link, and Tracy gave these presentations her full attention. As expected, the final three sessions at times lacked the depth and quality of the first three, but overall they were actually pretty good. Strangely good.

Tracy had to admit the work was quite a bit better than she'd seen in previous weeks. She was pleasantly surprised and wondered to herself what had changed all of a sudden.

When discussion time rolled around, the answer to Tracy's question became clear. It seemed like Lisa paid no attention whatsoever to the other presentations. She was totally preoccupied with her own work and almost seemed to be dozing off during the discussion. Brent, on the other hand got involved, albeit in a very negative way. On several occasions, he made harsh comments and was extremely critical about the quality of the code he was seeing. At times it seemed more like grandstanding than constructive criticism. Tracy could see her staff growing increasingly uncomfortable and upset.

But when it came time for Harry to participate the entire dynamic changed.

"Guys, let's take a step back for a second." Harry prepared to offer some perspective. "This has come a long way since we last met. You guys deserve a lot of credit for your work," he complimented.

"It's still not as clean as it should be," fired back Brent, who was never going to back down.

"But it's definitely moving in the right direction; wouldn't you agree, Brent?" Tracy interrupted for the first time all standup.

"Umm, yeah, I guess," said Brent, who was smart enough to know went he was beaten.

"Good, because I'm proud of the progress I'm seeing. And thank you to everyone who helped make it happen." She was staring strangely at Harry as she made her final point.

A Pre-Stand-Up Sit-Down

What none of the other managers had taken notice of was that in the days leading up to the session, Harry had made a point of meeting with the weaker groups. He had noticed in previous stand-ups that their work was not quite at the level of the other teams. And so he had offered his assistance to help them prepare for the latest stand-up session. He had been cautious not to seem overbearing, and the teams had gratefully accepted his help.

Unlike Lisa and Brent, who were myopically focused on their own work, Harry had put a real plan into place designed to give him a shot at the director role. Harry knew he had to distinguish himself in some way from his peers. And because he couldn't do it with superior coding he wanted to make sure he painted himself as a leader in Tracy's mind. He hoped his boss would notice how much value he could bring in raising the overall quality of the product and team. He was right.

So while Harry's rivals lobbed criticisms or ignored the other presentations, Harry did his best to be helpful. He had made several very complimentary observations and offered on numerous occasions to help them further so they could take it to the next level. For Tracy, who, like many executives, was overworked and felt burdened by her weaker team members, Harry's unsolicited leadership was like a gift from heaven. This was exactly the kind of leader she was looking for.

Later that afternoon, Tanya gathered the management team together for a quick meeting. Her decision had been made.

She started by thanking the team. "Guys, I know we've all been through a lot together in the past nine months. It's been hectic for all of us and I want to thank you for your maturity and leadership as we take our team to the next level." Her message was received with smiles and nods around the room.

She continued, "As we enter the next phase of our growth, we're going to need to rely heavily on our best leaders. And so I'm introducing the role of director of engineering. This person will report directly to me and manage all the development teams. After careful consideration, I'd like to congratulate our very own Harry on his promotion. Congratulations Harry, director of engineering!"

Your Personal Playbook: Don't Hold People Accountable

We learned a lot from the stories of Dottie and Harry. I personally fell victim to Dottie's trap several times early in my career. For a lot of talented managers, it's easy to get frustrated when your subordinates or peers don't pull their weight. In Dottie's case she just couldn't control her desire to hold people accountable for their inferior work even when it wasn't the best strategy for her own career advancement. What we learned from Harry is how critical it is to first choose the best strategy for winning and then implement it accordingly. Blindly holding people accountable or being hard on your peers and staff isn't always the optimal play. Don't lose sight of your primary objective at work—career advancement. Here are a few tips that will ensure you stay focused on helping people instead of holding them accountable:

- Define your power. An easy first step is to determine whether or not you have legitimate power over a person or group. If they work for you, you have power. If they don't, you don't. Your power situation dictates whether helping or holding accountable makes sense for you.

- Embrace empathy over emotion. Many people do not respond well to being held accountable. I find it more effective with many people I work with to offer help rather than criticism even when deep down inside I want to tear my hair out.

- Make it public. It doesn't help you career much to mentor people if nobody important will ever find out. Find ways to let influencers know that you're offering mentorship and support to your peers so you can benefit from the image of leadership when the time comes.

Chapter 5

Checkpoint: Your New Career Perspective

We've covered a lot of concepts so far in the book. Now we need to start putting them together in a pragmatic way. We've seen how real corporations work and how Incompetent Executives use specific tactics to exploit them. The key for us is to steal only their most effective tactics for our own game plans. Before we assemble our strategy, let's start with a quick summary of what we now know.

Your Playing Field: The Imperfect Corporation

Despite how they are portrayed in the media, on Wall Street, and in the countless success stories we hear every day, all companies are inherently flawed. We imagine corporations to operate with logic and order and fairness. They don't. We want to believe meritocracies abound, and hard work, intelligence, and reliability are the stepping-stones to success. They are not. We tell ourselves results orientation and passion will bring us closer to our career objectives. They can't.

What we often under-appreciate is that corporations are comprised of human beings, and all human beings are motivated by their personal security and fulfillment. So although we might window-dress the imperfect humanity of corporations with stock programs and SMART objectives and missions and visions, we know that companies are ultimately driven by human forces. The corner offices and executive boardrooms in real companies are not reserved for the smartest or the hardest working.

There is a little-known set of tactics every manager needs to incorporate into his or her career game plan to fully exploit the realities of corporate dynamics. Changes must be made to your priorities and personal scorecards to ensure you're focusing on the activities that will actually get you ahead. Embrace the imperfection of your organization or relegate yourself to Smart-but-Stationary status and watch your less-competent peers pass you by.

The Players: 3 Key Profiles

Corporations may be comprised of countless types of people with varying skills and personalities and agendas, but for our purposes we can safely group managers into three profiles: Smart-but-Stationary Managers, Incompetent Executives, and Lost Souls. This is the cast of characters you need to be concerned about.

The Smart-but-Stationary group is near and dear to my heart, and many of you will find yourselves in this profile. These are the intelligent, hardworking managers who can never seem to get ahead despite their best efforts. They have all the potential in the world but need to make adjustments to their career strategies to realize the success they deserve.

The second group, the Incompetent Executives, possesses none of the classical skills we associate with success. However, they are experts in the dark arts of career management. This is why the corner offices in your company are filled with so many people who seem to be incompetent yet inexplicably successful. Rather than belittle the Incompetent Executive, we study them. Our playbook steals the best from their career strategies for our own.

Finally, the Lost Souls. These are the pawns in the game and have little to teach you other than behaviors to avoid at all costs.

Understanding the players in the game is a big step toward putting your new strategy into action. Take a look around your company and put each person you work with into one of these three categories. It will help focus your networking and promotion activities on the right people. Perform an honest assessment of yourself, identify your own profile, and take the necessary steps to improve.

Your Playbook: 7 Tactics for Career Success

After many years of observation and analysis I've hand-picked the top seven principles to manage your career the right way. These are lessons taken straight from the playbooks of executives who succeed in spite of their glaring lack of skill, work ethic, and intelligence. When combined with your talent and skill, they'll make you unstoppable. We've reviewed a number of common career scenarios where the so-called Incompetent Executives come out on the winning side of the game despite their inherent limitations. The key for us is to incorporate those strategies into our own playbooks so we can play and win in the imperfect corporation.

1. Never Be Passionate About Your Ideas

Many of us have dreams of being transformative figures, and we are drawn to icons like Steve Jobs and Mark Zuckerberg for their passion and perseverance. But for every Jobs there are hundreds of bodies lined up along the road that tried and failed to execute a passion-based strategy. In my experience a reputation for objectivity is much more useful than a reputation for passion. The only surefire way to do that is to commit to providing very objective alternatives in every scenario rather than to drive at any one agenda or idea. As great as your ideas may seem to you, "you" are irrelevant. The only thing that matters is "what." Focus on helping your company evaluate ideas objectively and avoid passionate pursuits.

2. Embrace the Changes Everyone Else Hates

Because human beings are naturally opposed to change, the greatest moments for career advancement come in times of uncertainty and disruption. During these periods, like in an acquisition or management shakeup, the opportunities are at their greatest and your competition is at its worst. While your competitors are rebelling to change and worrying what the future may hold, you need to be executing your advancement strategy. It's critical to have a change playbook ready so you can capitalize on these moments when they present themselves.

3. Learn to Promote Your Projects

It's easy to fall into the trap of assuming your work speaks for itself, especially when you're busy. As managers, we often prioritize the work and deprioritize internal promotion during crunch time. This is a recipe for career disaster. It makes the false assumption that people in your organization, especially those outside your department, define success the same way you do. We know that corporations are driven by human priorities. Demonstrating to influencers in your company how your work will benefit them is much more important than the work itself. Strategically architecting an environment for success by promoting your projects before, during, and after launch is the real key to success. Doing so effectively can often make up for inferior work and act as an insurance policy for project failures.

4. Avoid the Farce of Results Orientation

Despite what your manager tells you or what the career blogs may say, a myopic focus on results can be a prison sentence for your career. We know from studying Incompetent Executives that it's much more productive to broaden your skill set than it is to fixate on short-term objectives. The challenge we face as managers is the burden of separating our own personal objectives (i.e., career advancement) from the company's objective (i.e., achieving performance results). Your career is much better served in the long run by expanding your expertise than by reliably delivering results for the organization. It should go without saying this is a matter of degrees. You need to do the minimum amount of results delivery to stay in the game long enough for your advancement strategy to pay off. Abandoning results altogether is equally unwise.

5. Don't Be a Part of the Herd

It's very comforting and often therapeutic to gripe and gossip with peers at work. We are naturally drawn to this behavior especially in times of change and uncertainty. You should never do it. We also tend to network with people at our own level or below in the company because it's comfortable and easy. It's a waste of time. To actually get ahead in a corporation you need to differentiate yourself from your competitors.

Gravitating to the herd has the opposite effect. Next time you feel tempted to gossip or gripe with your fellow peers, don't do it. Instead, create a tactical influencer plan and execute it. We'll go over how in the next section.

6. Find *Big* Problems to Solve

As it pertains to career advancement, small wins and reliable performance do not put a winning score on the board. It can take as many as five small victories to equal one big win. Managers who play a game based on reliability tend to become known only for their mistakes. Mistakes, unlike small wins, reverberate across the company and garner lots of attention. It makes much more sense to pursue a big-win strategy even at the expense of making more small mistakes. Big wins are memorable, they build attention outside your department, and they often don't need to come at a high risk to you personally.

7. Don't Hold People Accountable

Holding people accountable is another modern career principle we've allowed to spiral out of control. Whereas it makes perfect sense why the corporate entity benefits from employees and managers holding each other accountable, it makes almost no sense for your own career advancement. In my experience, there is much more to be gained by being seen as a mentor than as a task master. In practice people gravitate to, hire, and promote individuals they like to be around, not people who demand accountability. What's more, acts of mentorship build an image of leadership and make people want to work with and for you. Acts of discipline build a tactical image that runs counter to the leadership image that will ultimately get you promoted.

———

With these fundamentals clear in our minds, let's get to our action plan.

Chapter 6

Action: What You Can Do Tomorrow to Get Ahead

Getting to the next level in your career sometimes seems like a marathon. It can take two or three or more years to advance even one level. This is why so many of us operate in our daily jobs without a winning strategy. It's actually much easier to focus on short-term results and to fixate on the minutiae of our routines. We gravitate toward this path of least resistance because it feels better. In my experience, you have to play the long game to make your career take off fast. It sounds counterintuitive, but it's true. The good news is you can start immediately.

My goal in this chapter is to give you a set of tasks you can implement on Monday morning that will profoundly improve your career prospects and won't take several years to see a return on your investment. Here is a simple checklist of tasks that will get you on the right track and can be done in a single day:

- ⟲   Make an influencer plan.
- ⟲   Build a decision framework.
- ⟲   Create a promotion plan.
- ⟲   Assemble a learning calendar.
- ⟲   Create a change playbook.
- ⟲   Find a big project.
- ⟲   Identify someone to help.

Make an Influencer Plan

The influencer plan is a vital tool for every active career-management strategy. This is one of those tools that, when I talk about it, everyone nods and agrees at its obvious usefulness. But then very few people go through the motions of actually writing one down. Don't make this mistake. Take 10 minutes today and jot down a list of everyone in your company who has an influence over your career. This can include your boss, his or her boss, some key peers, and people from other departments who depend on your work. Even certain customers or business partners can find their way on this list if they can affect your upward mobility. Err on the side of having too many influencers, and be creative about how you assess who can influence your success or failure.

Here are seven criteria I use to determine whether or not an individual is an influencer for me:

1. **Seniority.** This person is more senior in the organization than I am.

2. **Risk.** This person can terminate my employment or influence my termination.

3. **Power.** This person can promote me or influence my future promotion.

4. **Exposure.** This person tends to be very vocal in the company and is listened to by many people.

5. **Fear.** This person has a tendency to be critical or negative and can be hard to work with.

6. **Validation.** Public support from this person would be good for my career.

7. **Future.** This person has proven to be going places and is likely to get promoted soon.

For each of these seven criteria we should assign a score between 1 and 5 to rank the degree of influence they have. Then we can total them up and see who to give priority to in our plan.

Now that we've made a list of criteria we can put it into a simple table and start filtering our potential influencers through it. I use something that looks like Figure 1 shown on page 184.

Notice when you apply a more comprehensive set of criteria, like I have done in Figure 1, seniority stops being the only determining factor of influence. We have to consider a variety of factors when assessing who we should be tactically influencing. In practice your list may be longer than mine. Yours may include many individuals from other departments as well as your own. You'll notice in my list that the most influential person to my career at this time was the VP of sales even though I was in the marketing department. That's primarily because he had a tendency to be very critical of the work delivered

Figure 1: Sample Influencer List and Ranking

												My Influencer List
Name	Title	Relationship	Seniority	Risk	Power	Exposure	Fear	Validation	Future	Total	Rank
Fred Brown	VP Marketing	My boss	4	5	5	2	2	4	3	25	2
Jeff Smith	VP Sales	My boss's peer	4	2	3	5	5	5	5	29	1
Melanie Green	VP Products	My boss's peer	4	2	2	3	4	4	3	22	4
Brian Jackson	Sales Director	My peer	2	1	1	5	5	5	5	24	3
Gavin Reid	Partner Manager	One level below me	1	0	0	4	5	2	3	15	5

by other departments. Validation from him would reverberate across the company. So would his criticism. As a result, I focused a lot of my time promoting my work to him prior to delivering it. I believed his endorsement and support were more important than the quality of the work itself. In this case, I was proved right and ultimately went on to get promoted and transferred to his department.

This brings us to the second part of the influencer equation: the influencer plan. The obvious question is: Once you know who you need to influence, how do you actually go about influencing them? The answer ties back into everything we've covered thus far. I like to look at the influencer plan as containing two parts. The first part is about long-term influence development, and the second part is about tactical project influence. We spoke extensively about project influence and the need to do active promotion before, during, and after any significant project you take on. An influencer plan in this case protects us against project failure and accounts for the human side of the corporation.

Long-term influence development, on the other hand, is about separating yourself from the herd and strategically networking with your key influencers on an ongoing basis. You can think of it as influence for the long game. This type of networking can often make managers uncomfortable, as they see it as butt-kissing or sucking up to senior people in the organization. Don't fall into this trap. I spent at least a decade of my career making fun of the butt-kissers and joking with my peers about how pathetic it was. I thought it was beneath me. Of course, I also spent a considerable amount of time griping as I saw the same people I made fun of rising in the ranks with promotion after promotion while I stayed stagnant. Influencer development, even upward on the organizational chart, can be done with tact, and is a tried and true method of effective networking.

The simplest way to get started is to take your prioritized list of influencers and create an influencer calendar. Essentially this is a reminder to set up a meeting at least once a quarter for influencers more senior than you and at least once a month for people at the same level as you. When it comes time for the actual meetings I tend to focus on basic relationship building and do my best to avoid making it all about business or overly professional. Ultimately, you need to be building human relationships with these people to exact any meaningful influence over them. People want to be around individuals who they like spending time with. As we know, this directly translates into who gets hired and promoted. The only other thing you want to cover when you meet with your influencers beyond personal relationship-building is to clearly understand their most important priorities. Once you understand what motivates people, you can find opportunities to help them.

I feel compelled to add that this is the point where people often start thinking, *Does this guy seriously expect me to make a list and book meetings with my boss's boss to kiss up?* Yes, I do. But you don't have to be insubordinate or overly aggressive to do it. You're not asking for anything or flattering them or trying to close them on something. You're just building a relationship and understanding their priorities. The rest will naturally take care of itself. Whether you like it or not, this is how people get ahead in corporations and if you're not going to do it you can be certain one of your competitors will. This is one of those key moments when it pays to think like an Incompetent Executive. They don't worry about how they're perceived by their peers and whether or not people will think they're sucking up; they're winners, and use every available tactic to get ahead. Be like them.

Make your influencer plan tomorrow and put into action one of the most powerful tools in your arsenal. Incompetent Executives do it all the time and get ahead in spite of themselves. Imagine what will happen when a talented manager like you starts using it, too.

Build a Decision Framework

The decision framework is a great tool to have on hand and you can build one in 15 minutes tomorrow morning. You'll be able to use it over and over again, and it will help you build an image of objectivity. I look for any chance I get to remind people how objective I am. When I'm delivering a new strategy or idea I could care less about what approach the company takes. And I certainly don't pretend to know whether or not one strategy is more likely to work than another.

As we saw in a couple of our tales, hubris often gets in the way of objectivity, and we make the mistake of backing our own ideas to a fault. Backing any one idea is too high risk and assumes both that you know the best course of action, and even if you do, that other people will agree with your assessment. Presenting a balanced and thoughtful decision-making framework is the smarter approach for your career. Helping others evaluate the decision collaboratively is a much safer tactic to any new strategy or idea even though it won't necessarily result in a better decision being made. It has the impact of distributing blame when things go badly, but in my experience does very little to diminish the credit you will get if the strategy is successful. Moreover, if you craft the decision-making framework effectively, you can often lead a team to the optimal decision anyway.

Figure 2 on pages 190 and 191 depicts a sample decision-making framework that can be used for almost anything. I probably use this two or three times a quarter and it never fails me. Notice how there is nothing in the section called "Decision Recommendation." You leave that blank, and lead the team or committee to decide on that collaboratively. The model is very easy to use. It has five sections:

Decision Context:

> This is just a couple of sentences to set the context for decision-making. You need to present the situational assessment and any factors that your audience needs to consider in evaluating alternatives.

Decision Constraints:

> This is the most important part of the framework. In this section you identify the key objectives, which any prudent course of action needs to satisfy. By taking this approach you are not backing any particular path or idea, but rather backing a thoughtful methodology. The former makes you seem overly passionate and emotional, the latter makes you seem objective and analytical.

Decision Alternatives:

> This is a simple section in which you identify two to three possible alternative courses of action. The only thing to keep in mind is to make sure you include only serious alternatives. The entire framework can backfire on you if you only include one reasonable option and a couple other bogus ones. Again, make sure you're being objective. People can smell a rigged decision framework a mile away.

Alternative Scoring:

> I usually set up this simple scoring table with the options running across the top and the constraints running down the left. I leave the actual scores blank and lead the team to assign scores of between 1 and 5 for each one. It should go without saying that the act of leading people through this exercise simultaneously creates an image of leadership for you and aligns them to any decision that ultimately gets made. Because they were part of the process in the first place it acts as an insurance policy against failure.

Decision Recommendation:

> This is just a space reserved to enter whichever decision the group ultimately aligns to. It's useful to have this there in case you need to later send it around to executives or prove that you went through a thoughtful process to make the decision.

Figure 2: Sample Decision-Making Framework

Japanese Go-to-Market Strategy—Decision-Making Framework
Decision Context:
The company is faced with a decision on how best to enter the Japanese marketplace. The opportunity has been sized at $40 million over the next five years. The key decision point now is: What is the best go-to-market approach to maximize profit and control risk?
Decision Constraints:
The correct strategic course must meet the following constraints to be a viable path for the company.   1. LEVERAGE. It must leverage our existing partnerships in the region.   2. CONFLICT AVOIDANCE. It cannot create channel conflict with our existing routes to market.   3. ROI. It must return a minimum of 10% in the first year.   4. MARGINS. It must deliver sustainable margins of 65% or more.   5. TIME TO MARKET. It must provide significant first mover advantage over competitors.
Decision Alternatives:
There are two feasible alternatives the company must consider for expansion to Japan.   1. Rapid expansion using *direct* channels to market.   2. Measured expansion using *indirect* channels and partners.

Sample Decision-Making Framework

Alternative Scoring:		
Constraints	Option 1: Direct	Option 2: Indirect
LEVERAGE	0	0
CONFLICT AVOIDANCE	0	0
ROI	0	0
MARGINS	0	0
TIME TO MARKET	0	0
Total	0	0
Decision Recommendation:		
For discussion.		

Keep this tool on hand in a spreadsheet or draw it up real time on a whiteboard. It's easy to use and works every time. You never have to worry about knowing the right answer ever again. Incompetent Executives have been milking it all the way to the bank for years. It's your turn now.

Create a Promotion Plan

The promotion plan is frankly just as simple as it sounds. And I won't overcomplicate it. You'd be surprised how many managers and young executives don't have a target promotion or promotions in mind at all times. And for the few who do, they often aren't creative enough in the possible promotions they might be able to get. I've never been handed a promotion in my entire career; it's very rare. So if you're sitting around waiting for someone to appreciate your work so much that he presents you with a promotion, you are making a colossal mistake. That is the very definition of a passive career-management strategy, if it can even be considered a strategy at all.

As I've said so many times, your only priority at work is to advance your career. That is how you attain your personal objectives for your personal shareholders—your family and loved ones. Everything else at work is secondary to this. The only way to attain your personal objectives, like more money, better benefits, vacation time, retirement savings, and other rewards, is to get promotions and move up the corporate ladder. I'll assume anyone who doesn't care about these things stopped reading a long time ago. So if your goal is to get promoted, you need to start with a promotion plan. It looks something like Figure 3 shown on page 193.

Figure 3: Sample Promotion Plan

Currently: Junior Associate Product Manager					
Promotion	Influencer 1	Influencer 2	Influencer 3	Primary Gap	Learning Action
Associate Product Manager	VP Product Management	Product Manager: John S.	Marketing VP: Kate M.	Ability to build good requirements docs	Jan: Pragmatic Marketing course
Content Marketing Manager	Director Content Marketing	Content Manager: Jane P.	VP Product Management	Experience writing technical blogs	Jan: Blog writing best practices
Manager, Product Support	Director, Customer Experience	VP Product Management	Support Specialist: Dave C.	Product troubleshooting	Jan: One week support ride-a-long

The promotion plan starts with identifying your promotion targets. Usually there are between one and three possible promotions you can be working toward at any given time. I would recommend you think creatively about this and extend your set of targets beyond your current department or business unit.

Once you've identified your promotion targets you need to clearly identify the influencers who can help or hinder your ability to get the promotion. You should have this already in the influencer plan we built earlier.

The final step is to speak to each of the key influencers A) to make your intentions clear that you are working toward this promotion, B) to understand what it will take to get there, and C) to request their regular feedback along the journey. Many managers feel this type of approach is tacky or butt-kissing, or they're afraid to do it. They couldn't be more wrong. When you speak to your influencers about a promotion, you're not asking to be promoted and you're not dictating a timeline. You're only making it known that you're after the promotion and willing to work for however long it takes to achieve it. This is the only way to make sure you understand what gaps you need to fill or what changes you need to make to be considered. Even if you're miles away from being ready, it's still very valuable to understand exactly how far and what steps are required to ultimately get there. You would be surprised how many people don't get promoted simply because nobody knew they were working toward it. A lot can be gained just by lobbying support from your influencers to help you improve. Everyone respects that type of ambition and you'll never get a negative reaction.

The final step in the promotion plan is to link it to your learning calendar. We'll explore this more in the next section, but needless to say, you need to set specific learning milestones for each possible promotion so you'll be closing the gaps between where you are today and where you need to be to get promoted.

This is another one of those tactics that everyone nods to but nobody actually does—nobody, with the exception of the Incompetent Executives getting promoted all the time. Make a point of going through these steps and actively managing your promotion plan.

Assemble a Learning Calendar

The learning calendar is a tool I use to force myself to actually work on broadening my skill set. It's closely connected to many of the other tools we'll also be putting into action. Without a learning calendar I find it too easy to deprioritize this vital aspect of my career plan. It is not enough to build deeper expertise in a single subject matter area, either. As we've seen in several of our stories, being a specialist doesn't lead to career advancement—career security perhaps, but definitely not advancement.

It's vital to document your learning curriculum and agenda at least a month at time and align it to your promotion and influence plans. I like to start by selecting three themes for the quarter and focus in on one per month. At least two of the three learning themes will be outside my established area of expertise. An example of a simple learning calendar you can use is shown on page 196.

The tendency is to keep going deeper and deeper into subjects we're already good at. It's easier that way, but it's a mistake. If you're already an expert in pricing models, don't invest your valuable time becoming the world's greatest pricing guy;

Figure 4: Sample Learning Calendar

My Learning Calendar					
Period: Q1 2014					
Promotional Goal	Learning Objective	Learning Theme	Learning Type	Month	Status
Associate Product Manager	Ability to build good requirements documents	Product Requirements Best Practices	Core	January	Completed
Content Marketing Manager	Experience writing technical blogs	Blog Writing Best Practices	Adjacent	February	In Progress
Manager, Product Support	Deep product troubleshooting knowledge	Our Technology Common Fixes	Adjacent	March	Not Started

it won't pay off for you in the end. How many CEOs out there were promoted to the top because they were pricing experts? So if you have pricing expertise already, I suggest focusing your learning themes on adjacent areas like licensing, channel models, and distribution mechanics. This way you are broadening your skill set within adjacent subjects, and painting an image of someone who could manage a larger team and hold wider accountabilities. By building this broader set of skills and creating an image of competency around several subjects, you'll get shortlisted for more promotion opportunities, which ultimately will translate to advancement for you.

Once you've identified the learning themes you're going to tackle for the quarter and connected them to your promotion goals, the next step is to actually assign time to learning. This is harder than it sounds. In my experience, many managers actually assign zero time to skill set expansion because they are so burdened by delivering on objectives and completing short-term projects. So you have to find a way to force yourself to learn something every day that will improve your skill set. I like to do this first thing in the morning because I have more energy and I can find fewer excuses not to do it. I'll set aside 30 minutes each morning to read up on my subject themes. If I'm particularly busy or tired I'll watch videos or listen to podcasts instead. I recommend setting up your blog RSS feed with the top bloggers in each subject area you're pursuing. You'll have a permanent library of reference material for as long as you need it.

The last point to make with respect to the learning calendar is that you need to tell people you're doing it. Learning and not telling people about it is pointless for you career strategy. Sure, it's great to broaden your skill set but if nobody knows, you'll just be the smartest low-level manager in your company. I look for opportunities to tell my influencers about things I've learned recently as a topic of conversation. It's always a great approach to mention what you've recently learned and ask for guidance or advice from their experience or from what they know of the subject area. That way you're not just bragging about how smart you are and rather asking for help or perspective.

The Incompetent Executive gets promoted because so often he or she carries a shallow knowledge of many subjects—the Jack of All Trades. Start expanding your expertise and steal their tactic for your own game plan.

Make a Change Playbook

Periods of organizational turmoil are your best opportunity for career advancement. It's in these moments that the big moves in your career will be made. I find it helpful to document my game plan when I see big changes coming. The process of actually writing my plan down helps to remind me how important it is to be consciously executing purposeful tactics during these periods versus reacting emotionally. Unlike the influencer plan, you don't need a structured spreadsheet or model for this one. You can just doodle these in a notebook to make sure you're not forgetting your plan.

I recently met with a business partner who confided in me within an hour of meeting him that he had a new boss he couldn't stand. He just couldn't figure out how to deal with him, and he and the rest of the team missed their old boss immensely. As much as he delivered the polite version of his plight, it was pretty obvious that he and his peers were not handling this change scenario well. A management change is almost universally mishandled by staff who fight against what has already taken place in some naïve hope their discontent can actually reverse time. In this case, when your peers are all gossiping and griping about the evil new boss, you should be actively networking with her and finding ways to be helpful in the transition. Getting on the winning side of change is as much about choosing to play on the winning team as it is about any specific strategy. Having a positive attitude and aligning yourself with the eventual winners are your keys to success.

So when change is afoot, I jot down a few key notes in three basic areas to guide my behaviors. It reminds me that my goal is to get ahead in the company and not to express my emotions or misgivings about the situation. Here is a sample of what that might look like:

Figure 5: Sample Change Playbook

My Change Playbook

Change: Marketing and Sales Merging

1. Reassess my influencer list:
   VP of sales is now in charge. Need to add him to my list.

2. Identify transition projects:
   Volunteer for team process alignment committee.

3. Key actions:
   Book lunch with VP of sales. Book kickoff meeting with sales directors.

The first area I focus on is the influencer list. It has most likely evolved as a result of the change that has occurred. I make a quick list of who the key players are and who can most profoundly influence my success or failure in the new environment. My only caution is not to let any personal misgivings cloud your assessment of who actually has power and influence. Sometimes we can convince ourselves power hasn't shifted when in fact it has.

The second thing I take note of is what key transition projects are likely to take place or have been scheduled already. I want to be a part of these and will do whatever I can to participate. These will come in the form of process alignment meetings, systems integrations, best practice sharing, and a variety of other events. They all have the goal of smoothing the transition from the old way to the new way. You will participate on these committees and in these meetings ostensibly to help in the transition, but in reality you're tactically demonstrating leadership and networking with the winning team.

The final area I make note of is how I can advance my position during the change period. Specifically, what I will do to proactively improve my status. This can include things like booking a meeting with the new boss to understand her priorities and challenges. It might be taking one or two new people out for lunch or dinner after an acquisition. It can be the small things and casual conversations that reveal the best opportunities for career advancements in a highly dynamic environment. If you see yourself doing the same old routine trying to ignore the chaos around you, you should stop and get involved.

The most important thing in taking advantage of change scenarios is your attitude. Get on the winning team. Do the opposite of what the herd is doing. Find opportunities to demonstrate leadership in the face of disruption, which will often be present during these times. This is a great example of when the Incompetent Executive performs well while others do not. Get strategic during turmoil and rise to the top.

Find a *Big* Project

This one doesn't require a lot of additional discussion. As we've covered, it's the big wins that create upward mobility in a company. Your best case playing a strategy based on reliability is job security. Often when I tell people to go out and find a big project they respond with a look that says *but my job doesn't require any big projects.* This is exactly the kind of cop-out we use to excuse our lack of success. There is always a big project to find. Fix something. Propose something. Contribute to someone else's project. The key here is to be a part of something that will create attention and interest, and demonstrate you are a leader. Just don't get too passionate about any one strategy or path. Be objective; present the company options with how to improve or develop or advance. Attaching yourself to big projects is so important it almost doesn't even matter if the project itself is a success or failure. It's about being seen as a leader. Often these projects will feel like a burden. They'll be outside your objectives. Do them anyway.

Identify Someone to Help

To get ahead, your superiors need to be able to imagine you at the next level. One of the best ways to do it is to be seen mentoring and helping your peers in the organization. You can start doing this tomorrow. I look for the opportunities when most people hold their peers accountable or criticize them. Instead of holding them accountable, I offer my help and support. And I do it publicly. This takes a lot of emotional control because often the best situations for helping people are ones where someone's incompetence has impaired your ability to get a project executed or task completed.

Make a list of a few peers and one or two subordinates who routinely struggle to execute their work effectively. Make sure your list has more peers than subordinates. Helping peers is much more powerful than helping subordinates, because you're already expected to be doing the latter. The people on this list are the ones all the other managers complain about. The ones who hold up projects, or submit work late or with low quality. Instead of making life hard on them like everyone else does, you're going to find specific opportunities to make life easier for them. Then you're going to make sure everyone knows you did it. This is how you tactically build an image of leadership. Waiting for people to notice you have leadership qualities just takes too long.

This one can be done in your head, although I always recommend writing things down. I find it has the impact of driving me to action. A sample of something I might do is shown on page 203.

This is just a simple list; there's nothing fancy about it. But it helps. You'll often find Incompetent Executives are very helpful. It's one of the reasons they move up the corporate ladder. Add this simple task to your routine and watch your leadership image grow.

Figure 6: Sample Mentoring List

My Mentoring List

Objective:

Try to help these guys be successful. Let people know I'm doing it.

Eric M.:

Next time his deal review goes bad, pull him aside and show him how to build a proper sales deal summary. Make sure he uses my template.

Dan S.:

Help him fix his margin projections. He keeps confusing list price, street price, and wholesale price.

Dawson K.:

Give him a better management reporting dashboard. He's presenting too much information nobody cares about. Give him mine.

Conclusion

Your Wakeup Call:
Now, Make It Happen

If your career strategy is based on being smarter or working harder or reliably delivering results, you are making a big mistake. Being smarter is not the smartest way to get to the top. Working harder is the hardest way to advance your career. And reliable performance is the most reliable way I know to freeze your career in its tracks.

If you're anything like I was for the first 15 years of my career, you find yourself getting more frustrated with every passing year. You can't seem to get ahead in spite of your hard work and talent. You see other people having success, oftentimes in spite of glaring incompetence. You probably spend a lot of time wondering about the injustice of it all. *How can a smart person like me not be advancing my career while these Incompetent Executives seemingly get ahead with ease?*

The answer, as we've discussed, starts with a better understanding of the way corporations really work. They're not the mechanical, logical entities everyone assumes they are. They're flawed from top to bottom and are driven by human dynamics more than any notion of logic. Meritocracies do not exist in practice, and you can't depend on the company to notice your great work and reward you with promotions. A passive career strategy won't work for you. You need to take a more active approach to finding and capitalizing on the real opportunities for advancement.

Rather than bemoan the Incompetent Executives around you, you need to learn from them. I've given you a playbook from my own experiences that has proven to work and vaulted me from a talented-but-underappreciated young manager to an executive planted firmly in the corner office. But the path to the executive suite is not clean and neat like we hope it would be. This path wasn't built on reliability, hard work, and talent. It's built on opportunism and contrarian tactics. Getting to the corner office means you often have to do things that feel uncomfortable or will isolate you from your peers. It's uncomfortable, but it works.

The key to moving beyond hoping for success to actually reaping success is to reprioritize your focus when you're at work. Stop focusing on short-term objectives and tasks, and invest as much time and energy as you can on your career advancement playbook. Avoid the herd mentality at all costs. Start promoting your projects. Be at your best when difficult change is afoot and everyone around you is rebelling. Stop holding people accountable and start helping them to succeed. Choose to be objective over passionate when presenting ideas and strategies. And favor high-scoring projects over reliable performance of everyday tasks.

I've stolen these tactics straight from the pages of the Incompetent Executive's playbook. If they've helped these mediocre minds get to the top, imagine what they'll do for you. Start tomorrow to create your career advancement plan and watch as you rise up the ranks.

Appendix

Your New Career Playbook

Never Be Passionate About Your Ideas

Here are a few guidelines you can use to develop the extremely powerful image of objectivity. Incorporate them into your game plan and they'll never let you down.

- Always present options. Even if you're convinced you know the correct strategy, you must always present alternative courses of action. We're taught to do this in business school, but you rarely see it executed effectively in a high-paced corporate setting.

- Don't present fake options. Presenting bogus options in hopes of stacking the deck in favor of your idea is a rookie move. If you can't think of other strategic options to present, you are probably overly passionate about your own concept. People can see through fake options and it only makes you look immature.

- Learn to embrace any decision. It takes maturity to embrace options you don't personally favor. But in the career game, that kind of objective, professional approach will win you way more points than any one big idea you may have. Be prepared to enthusiastically embrace whatever strategic path the most influential people ultimately align with.

Embrace the Changes Everyone Else Hates

Here are three quick tips that will make sure you embrace the changes everyone else hates and ultimately end up on top:

- Make a change plan. You need to actually write down what your plan is or your emotions will likely get the best of you. Jot down some tactics when a major transition occurs to force yourself to act strategically and not emotionally.

- Pick the winner with your mind, not your heart. Make an objective assessment of which side is likely to come out on top and join that team. If someone has just bought your company or has just taken over your department, choose that team. Don't fight against the winning side.

- Leave your ego at the door. If you execute the correct change playbook, people will make fun of you and tease you for being a suck-up. Ignore them. Your career is not about making friends; it's about advancement.

Learn to Promote Your Projects

Here are a few tips you can use to make sure you never forget that promotion is your number-one project priority:

- Know your influencers. Make sure you know the three to five people who have the most influence on your project's success and failure. Look for outspoken people and individuals who tend to be critical.

- Promote three times. Good promotion starts with getting people onside with the basic concept. Then it's about giving a sneak peek to bring critical people onto your team. Last, it's about objectively promoting the results for everyone to share in its success or failure.

- Promotion is the priority. When you get busy you'll be tempted to forego promotion. It's much safer to sacrifice the work instead. Invest what little time you have in preparing your audience and taking the risk out of the presentation.

Avoid the Farce of Results Orientation

Here are three key tactics you can add to your career strategy that will ensure you properly invest your time and energy at work:

- Reallocate your time. Favor skills expansion over results delivery. Spend 20 to 30 percent of everyday learning new skills with the intention of broadening your expertise versus specializing in any one area.

- Expand your perceived position. Make a point of telling people what you're learning and the progress you're making. They need to be able to imagine you in other roles with wider responsibilities.

- Play the long game. Your career plays out over many companies and bosses. Never tie your future to one person or one skill set. In today's rapidly changing corporations you need to favor skill flexibility over skill depth.

Don't Be a Part of the Herd

Here are some can't-miss tips to make sure you never get stuck in the herd:

- Never be negative. It never pays to be negative about your colleagues or your boss. Even if you're surrounded by incompetence, you can't get anywhere by being negative. It may seem disingenuous at times, but you have to act positive at all times and about all people.

- Create an image of loyalty and respect. Find as many opportunities as you can to show deference and respect for your boss. These opportunities come up a lot if you're looking for them. Don't debate with your boss in public, but look for healthy debate opportunities in private.

- Focus on differentiating yourself from others. Don't ever forget your peers at work are your competition. They're not your friends—at least not in the game of career management. You need to be looking for ways to elevate yourself above other people on the team. A good first step is to spend more time with your boss and less time with your teammates.

Find *Big* Problems to Solve

Here are a few quick tips you can use to make sure you stay focused on a touchdown strategy for your career:

- Don't wait to be noticed. Nobody is watching you. Reliability is not a leadership quality. At least not one anybody cares enough about to promote you. The best way to get to the top is to make yourself more visible by taking on bigger projects. Even if that means you volunteer for projects that have nothing to do with your objectives.

- Wait for the right pitch. You can't just swing blindly for every big project that comes your way. You need to choose the ones with the highest probability for success. The ones that will connect you to your career influencers. Having a big project failure is as profoundly bad as having a big project success is good.

- Swing for the fences. Don't turn down chances to hit a home run. They come around more than we think sometimes. Next time your boss asks you to be a part of a project or to take something on outside of your objectives, say yes.

Don't Hold People Accountable

Here are a few tips that will ensure you stay focused on helping people instead of holding them accountable:

- Define your power. An easy first step is to determine whether or not you have legitimate power over a person or group. If they work for you, you have power. If they don't, you don't. Your power situation dictates whether helping or holding accountable makes sense for you.

- Embrace empathy over emotion. Many people do not respond well to being held accountable. I find it more effective with many people I work with to offer help rather than criticism even when deep down inside I want to tear my hair out.

- Make it public. It doesn't help you career much to help people if nobody important will ever find out. Find ways to let influencers know that you're offering mentorship and support to your peers so you can benefit from the image of leadership when the time comes.

Notes

Introduction

1. CAGR or Compound Annual Growth Rate is a business or investing term that provides a constant rate of return over a specific time period.

2. A scattergraph is a type of mathematical diagram using coordinates to display values for two variables for a set of data.

Chapter 1

1. Maslow's hierarchy of needs is portrayed in the shape of a pyramid with the largest, most fundamental levels of needs at the bottom and the need for self-actualization at the top.

2. A meritocracy is a system is based on perceived intellectual talent measured through examination and/or demonstrated achievement in the field in which it is implemented.

3. Patrick Lencioni is a business management author who is best known for "The Five Dysfunctions of a Team," a business fable that explores work team dynamics.

4. During the 1950s, psychologist Solomon Asch conducted a series of experiments designed to demonstrate the power of conformity in groups.

Chapter 4

1. The Bureau of Labor Statistics reports that people born between 1957 and 1964 held an average of 11 jobs from ages 18 to 44.

Index

About the Author

BRENDAN REID is an accomplished executive and author specializing in the too-often-ignored human side of corporate dynamics. As a consultant and keynote speaker, he has worked with the smallest start-ups and the largest corporations in the world. His uniquely personal perspective on career management makes him sought after as a coach and panelist.

Brendan lives in Toronto with his partner, Aya, and their three dogs.

To find out more about Brendan or to book him for speaking engagements, visit *www.brendanreid.com.*

To hear Brendan's insights and expertise on a daily basis, follow him on Twitter *@brendanmreid.*